FARMER
JANE

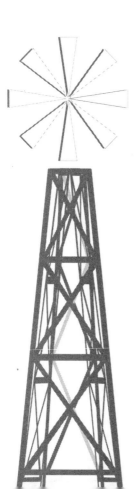

FARMER JANE

Women Changing the Way We Eat

Temra Costa

GIBBS SMITH
TO ENRICH AND INSPIRE HUMANKIND

FOR MY PARENTS AND
ALL OF THE FOOD- AND
FARM-LOVING WOMEN

First Edition
14 13 12 11 10   5 4 3 2 1

Published by
Gibbs Smith
P.O. Box 667
Layton, Utah 84041
1.800.835.4993 orders
www.gibbs-smith.com

Designed by Jocelyn Foye
Printed and bound in Canada

Gibbs Smith books are printed on either recycled, 100% post-
consumer waste, FSC-certified papers or on paper produced from
a 100% certified sustainable forest/controlled wood source.

Library of Congress Cataloging-in-Publication Data

Costa, Temra.
    Farmer Jane : women changing the way we eat / Temra Costa.
        p. cm.
    ISBN-13: 978-1-4236-0562-1
    ISBN-10: 1-4236-0562-4
    1. Women social reformers. 2. Food—United States. 3. Agricultural
information networks. 4. Farm produce—United States—Marketing.
5. Local foods—United States. 6. Community-supported agriculture—
United States. 7. New agricultural enterprises—United States. I. Title.
    HD9006.C718 2010
    338.1'973—dc22
                                    2009034912

CONTENTS

WOMEN'S ROLE IN THE SUSTAINABLE FOOD & FARMING MOVEMENT

This book is about the women behind the "delicious revolution" that's changing how we eat and farm in the United States. I often get asked why men weren't included in this book, and it's not that men *aren't* changing how we eat. Men are definitely involved—it's just that they're really good at getting all of the press. Women, on the other hand, have long been underrepresented in the public sphere about the sheer amount of work they do, at home and outside of the home, in food planning and preparation, while advocating for a healthier food system* and environment. They are our heroes of today through their everyday acts of living, by becoming the fastest growing number of diversified farmers in the country, controlling the majority of household spending, dominating nonprofits dedicated to shifting the balance from conventional to sustainable foods, and through the creation of menus and businesses that reflect their socio-environmental values. This "delicious revolution," as Alice Waters would say, unfolds as we look at the life stories of thirty key women that are making a more sustainable food system—*the* solution to our health and environmental woes.

Yet our food system hasn't always required such advocacy or noise. After all, it's only been in the last century that our food and rural places have experienced the industrialization that is making us, and the land, sick. During this relatively short time, our food has gone awry, transitioning from a system that was almost entirely

---

* *Food system* refers to the chain of production, from farm to plate, that includes farm workers, farmers, distributors, buyers, policy makers, chefs, grocers, and others.

local, seasonal, and regionally appropriate, to the very literal "global supermarket" of today. Most often the fruits and vegetables of this global supermarket are devoid of flavor and provenance, and when paired with hormone-filled meats and dairy, processed junk food, and products from genetically engineered plants (namely corn, soy, and canola), these newfangled foods are the detriment of humanity and the natural world. The industrialization of our food may have been perceived to be a boon for people with limited incomes for a very brief moment, but we are starting to see the elephant in the room. Cheap, conventional (chemical) food abundance has led to the rise of obesity, diabetes, and other food-related health issues caused by improper diets. But health issues aside (they could fill an entire book), we have become disconnected from the very people and the land that we are *dependent* on to provide our very sustenance. We have lost sight of the fact that the fertility of the soil determines our vitality. But this, too, is starting to change.

BRINGING IT TO THE TABLE

Having not grown up on an all-local, organic, or even sustainable diet (minus the wild game and fish my father hunted and brought home), my learning curve was just the same as anyone else's. In the relatively food challenged climes of Wisconsin, my family and I didn't preserve foods or garden, nor were we aware of any farmers markets; it just wasn't a part of our lifestyle. My grandmother, on the other hand, did have today's coveted food preservation skills. I remember eating her pickles, jams, and other foods she had stocked for the winter. However, for me, and for most that have awakened to the impact of sustainable foods,** it took a special moment.

** *Sustainable food and agriculture* refers to food and farming that doesn't compromise the production capabilities or health of future generations. Such systems take the natural world into consideration, and view the positive health of the environment (soil, water, air, flora and fauna, mammals, etc.) as critical to achieving a truly sustainable food system.

My visceral moment of "getting it" was at age nineteen when I walked into the Williamson Street Cooperative in Madison, Wisconsin. The smells of seaweed, organic vegetables, fermented foods, sprouted granola, and whole grain bread were part of an entirely unknown food universe. These foods led me to wonder what the heck all the "other" foods were and where they came from. Once I started questioning the integrity of something as essential as food, there was no turning back.

After studying agriculture and advocating for sustainable foods while in college, I was fortunate to find a position with the Community Alliance with Family Farmers (CAFF). Living in California fueled my conviction that another type of eating experience was possible, as I dove into all of the great varieties that my new food culture had to offer: kadota figs, fuyu persimmons, mixed greens and collards, crenshaw melons, with each new season providing new discoveries. My farmers market purchases were supplemented by fruit trees growing around my house in the infamous Village Homes of Davis. What I couldn't get from either market or tree, I would buy at the Sacramento Natural Food Coop (one of the several dozen remaining member-owned food co-ops in the country). My grandmother was tickled when I would call her to get canning and jamming advice to put up some of my favorite fruits and veggies for the winter.

I learned that every time we buy food, we vote with our dollars for either chemical or non-chemical agriculture, for fair trade, or for seasonal foods, and soon I found myself spending upwards of 30 percent of my nonprofit salary by "voting with my fork." This wasn't an easy reality to swallow, but I continued to do so. As Jessica Prentice articulates in "Promoting Local and Seasonal Food," if people can afford cell phones, plasma TVs and $200 jeans and shoes, they can spend a little more money on their food—even if it's only $5 extra a week. So, admittedly, eating seasonally and sustainably does cost a bit more per pound. And this is ultimately an issue of public policy (the Farm Bill) and social justice. Food is such a common denominator that it is why these women have chosen to advocate for better food—seasonal, sustainable, and fresh—as their focal point in making the greatest impact on people's lives and the environment. The issue of food is one that cuts through ethnic boundaries to each of our stomachs. It's an issue that each of us vote on *every day*.

WOMEN AND FOOD

This book celebrates the results that we are starting to see due to women's efforts to change how our country eats and farms. Since 2002, we have started to see an increase in the number of farms in the country, the number of farmers markets and community supported agriculture programs, and the number of people who are concerned about where their food is coming from.[1]

Of the top fifteen national nonprofits focusing on sustainable agriculture issues, women comprise 61.5 percent of the employees and 60 percent of the executive directors.[2] As mothers of children, nurturers of health, and the ones in control of 85 percent of household budgets, women have the largest impact and concern when it comes to what they feed themselves and their families (oftentimes extending their generosity to their wider communities).[3] On the farm, women are one of the fastest growing demographics to own and operate farms in the United States, and they are tending towards diversified, direct-marketed foods that create relationships with eaters.[4]

Women are running successful food businesses too: restaurants, catering companies, and community-supported kitchens, to name a few. They are writing legislation and setting a new tone for policy, such as Michelle Obama's political act of sowing an organic garden in the White House lawn.

Each of the book's chapters focuses on the areas of change that women are leveraging to bring greater sustainability back to our plates. Every chapter features profiles of women and ends with Recipes for Action—ideas for how you as an eater, a farmer, or an owner/employee of a food business can join in.

These women's tales have plots and subplots that each could have entailed an entire book. And while the following topics were mentioned, they no doubt warrant more pages about their critical significance to proliferating sustainable agriculture in the U.S.: water, renewable energy, carbon farming, women of color, food deserts, general health and nutrition related to food (including obesity and diabetes), and the U.S. Department of Agriculture's programs.

The women of these pages are an inspiration to the ways that sustainable food and farming is again becoming a reality. But out there among the fields, organizations, and homes of America are the untold stories of women that are promoting the agenda for sustainability of our food. Visit www.farmerjane.org to post the stories of women who are heroes in your community and to connect with organizations involved in the food movement. Wherever you are, you too can be a woman (or man) that is helping change the way America eats and farms—one plate at a time.

CHAPTER 1

BUILDING NEW FARM-TO-EATER RELATIONSHIPS

As women farmers are taking the wheel of food production they are tending towards smaller, diversified, and direct-to-eater markets. Their CSAs, farmers markets, and sales to restaurants and other food businesses are especially creating stronger relationships between their fields and eaters.* These relationships are laying the foundation of our growing local and sustainable food economy that provides farmers with their livelihoods in exchange for the most essential ingredient of life—food. In our web 2.0 world, having a face behind our food is driving more people to spend their dollars on direct-marketed farm goods that are good for us and the environment. This is what's behind food business's shift to carrying such foods—the purchasing power we have. Every dollar we spend sends signals to the food buyers of the world.

Yet the shift towards a more regional and transparent food system is still challenging, as we tend towards convenience and lower prices. While local foods may appear (to some) to be more expensive than their conventional counterparts, it is really only a perceived price differential. Cheap food is "cheap" because of the hidden costs that we don't see reflected in the price, such as pollution, poor working conditions for food industry employees, poor treatment of the land, mistreatment of animals, and a massive distribution system with a huge petroleum footprint, not to mention rising food safety concerns.

* The word "eater" is used because "consumer" doesn't relay a relationship, but rather the action of a purchase; this word has removed the social aspect of what we purchase and eat and has degraded us to mere purchasers of products.

Dru Rivers, in this chapter, has observed firsthand that for many, prioritizing local food and knowing your farmer has become a more trustworthy source of food for many people. "The food scares that keep happening—spinach, tomatoes, peppers, almonds, you name it—are making CSA and direct buying from growers the answer to eating safer food," she says.

As eaters, we need to know where exactly our food is being produced and without imposing more cost on farmers. It's a question of food safety as much as it is of sustainability and creating vibrant local economies. Knowing where our food comes from helps us:

- eat from as close to home as possible;
- choose exceptional freshness and flavor;
- support our local community/economy;
- increase revenue for farmers (selling direct provides a higher return to farmers) so that they, and future generations, continue producing food;
- be more connected to seasonality, place, and varieties of foods that are grown in our region.

The women farmers in this chapter are taking the challenge to bring us more local foods by prioritizing new direct farm-to-eater relationships; they are bringing a face back to our food. And in providing the much-needed alternatives to the international and anonymous food found in our supermarkets, they are working to create a new food future for their communities built on trust, education, sustainability, and transparency. This is something more and more people are buying into—the decision to eat what they value and want to preserve.

NANCY VAIL

FARMER, PIE RANCH, PESCADERO, CALIFORNIA

Pie Ranch is committed to a more sustainable food system and social change, as well as educating youth about agriculture.

The name for Pie Ranch" says Nancy, "came from seeing an aerial photo of the 'upper slice'—where we live now, which resembles a slice of pie." Nancy and her husband, Jered, having worked with children, young adults, and farmers involved with sustainable agriculture, knew that pie would be a lure to engage people in thinking about food and farming issues. The "aha" moment for Nancy that would influence her goal to become a farmer happened while she was working at a farm that had adopted a CSA model. "Community Supported Agriculture, as a philosophy," Nancy realized, "went beyond the individualism of homesteading and created a context where eaters and producers can be in direct relationships."

This relationship is integral to the farm that Nancy started with her husband, Jered Lawson, and their friend Karen Heisler. Both a place and an organization, Pie Ranch is committed to a more sustainable food system and social change, as well as to educating youth about agriculture and showing them where the food they eat comes from.

VISITING PIE RANCH

The enticement begins with the "eat pie" neon sign beckoning from the roadside barn just south of Pescadero, off of Highway 1, that winding stretch of coastline that sails from the north to the southernmost tip of California. The road, a piece of black licorice with the Pacific's salty waves licking the shore, gets your mind drifting on the promise of warm fruit-filled pastries. Passing dunes and beaches, you start to think you might have missed the farm until a sign appears on the side of the road exclaiming, "Farm stand open—barn dance TONIGHT!" You've just arrived at Pie Ranch.

In addition to finding pie, produce, jam, and homemade pancake mix at the farmstand on weekends during the peak of growing season, one Saturday per month passersby can spend the afternoon participating in any number of authentic farm projects—harvesting berries, weeding the apple orchard, clearing brush from the fence lines, cleaning and boxing eggs. The monthly community workdays culminate in a potluck gathering and barn dance, a warm and rollicking event that the local rural community has come to rely on. This not-to-be-missed event routinely draws folks from as far away as San Francisco, Oakland, and San Jose.

"Pie brings everyone to the table and embodies environment, economics, social justice, and soul."

Guided by its educational mission and the theme of pie, the farm has designed its cropping system around ingredients for both sweet and savory kinds. With wheat grown as the foundational crop, the pie fillings grown include apples, strawberries, rhubarb, blackberries, raspberries, pumpkins, lemons, and limes. "In addition to pie ingredients," says Nancy, "we raise other crops and animals for their nutritional and educational value as a way to help illustrate how the foods our visitors consume gets from farm to table, such as milk from a cow, corn for flour and popping, legumes for fresh and dry beans, and cattle, goats, and chicken for meat."

The kids who come to Pie Ranch to learn about farming are usually high school students from the Bay Area, Pescadero, Santa Cruz, and different parts of the globe; however, the main focus is on providing the opportunity for repeat visits rather than one-time experiences alone. Nancy says, "We believe that repeat visits build upon themselves; youth connect to the land, to the staff, and to each other. Understanding and respect for the farm grow as youth experience the cycle of days, weeks, months, seasons, and years." Pie Ranch also offers yearlong apprenticeships and summer internships for people who are seriously interested in becoming farmers and gardeners. Monthly community workdays are opportunities to teach and engage the local community in food production, farming, and sustainability. Additionally, Pie Ranchers host monthly workshops on topics such as land tenure, gopher control, nutritionally dense crops, and animal husbandry (to name a few!).

The farm's newest family member, a personable and photogenic young Jersey Cow named Adelaide, will teach countless youth from the city that milk doesn't originate at the supermarket, but from a warm-blooded lactating mammal that should be treated with love. "Adelaide grazes on irrigated pasture blocks where strawberries once grew. Someday, many years from now, through a complex rotation schedule of annuals and pasture, the land will grow berries again," explains Nancy. This rotation of animals to various pastures is an integral practice to a sustainable farming system, one that has been used over the centuries in a cycle of sustainability.

Nancy explains that the pasturing of the animals—first cows, then chickens—allows for an "active rest" period before the next cycle of "extractive cropping" ensues. Perennial grasses are then planted to shade out the weeds while the land lays fallow and rejuvenates. "It's a crop rotation designed to last forever without the need for importing fertility and energy," says Nancy. "One of the benefits of being an educational farm is that it allows, even encourages, system integration on a small scale, something that the economic pressures of production farming unfortunately discourages." Taking their commitment to demonstrating the ecological benefits of whole-system integration seriously, Nancy knows that this system "has implications not just in farming but in all aspects of humans' relationship to natural resources."

DIGGING INTO FARMING

As a university student, Nancy's studies in history, her growing interest in the politics of food through volunteering with a cooperative restaurant, and her protestation of the Persian Gulf War provided some relief to the turmoil she felt as a member of society. Nancy remembers the questions she would ask herself at the time, "How do you live in this world in a way that's hopeful, direct, and authentic given the fact that so many things seem negative? How do you engage in the world in a way that makes sense? This is what started me in the direction of farming and food system change."

After some time teaching English in Japan and participating in the WWOOF program (World Wide Opportunities on Organic Farms) in

New Zealand, Nancy ended up on a journey farming her way across the States. She had read Helen and Scott Nearing's *The Good Life* and was intrigued by the path of homesteading, something she dabbled in while visiting the Nearings' homestead in Maine. It sounds like an existential reality she was living, as while scouting around, she happened to bump into Elliot Coleman on his tractor. Coleman and his wife, Barbara Damrosch, are leaders in sustainable agriculture practices and new methods of farming year-round at their farm, Four Seasons Farm—no small feat, considering Maine's winters. Nancy ended up apprenticing with them for a month before finding her way to Illinois and Angelic Organics, which began when farmer John Peterson adopted a diversified CSA model (an action that ended up literally saving his family farm). She fell completely in love with the farm life at Angelic Organics and learned from John that it is possible to embody vision and practice, hard work and celebration, dirt and sparkle. (See the film *The Real Dirt on Farmer John* for the full story.)

After working and playing hard in the flat fields of the Midwest, Nancy picked up and headed back East for the winter of 1996, this time to Hawthorne Valley Farm in New York's Hudson Valley. This farm gave her the experience of land through an array of enterprises, including a bakery, CSA, dairy, Visiting Students Program, farm store, and apprenticeships. Then, after moving back to California and completing an apprenticeship program at the Center for Agroecology and Sustainable Food Systems at UC Santa Cruz (see sidebar, page 18), Nancy had all the evidence she needed to answer her calling.

After that first year of the program, she stayed on as a second-year apprentice in the ten-acre field that the farm managed, and then a third year, all the while taking on more responsibility. At the time, the farm program had grown enough that it needed a second manager, and Nancy was the perfect candidate. Nancy ran the CSA (which Jered helped found when he was an apprentice in 1994) and taught field production farming alongside her mentor, Jim Leap, the CASFS farm manager. "It was a dream job for me, such an incredible place to be honing my farming skills, learning about production and the critical role that education plays, while engaged with the local community through the CSA."

Nancy loved her role as an educator, finding that while out in the field, "observation and learning by doing is key." It was a constant juggling act, teaching and inspiring people to thin a 600-foot-row crop of carrots while explaining to apprentices the complex interactions of seed, soil, water, and environmental conditions. Not to mention getting all the work done on time! During her time there, she contributed writing for the center's two training manuals, "Teaching Organic Farming and Gardening" and "Teaching Direct Marketing and Small Farm Viability." Additionally, Nancy was the Farm-to-College coordinator at CASFS from 2005 to 2008, a program through which she engaged university students in activities and classes at the campus farm and connected the campus farm and other local farms' produce with the campus dining halls. She spent a total of ten years at UCSC, then in 2003 moved onto Pie Ranch to begin what she considers her life's work of connecting people with the source of their food.

HOW THE PIE BEGAN

While Nancy and Jered didn't have the capital they needed to purchase Pie Ranch, they had a vision that they shared with their friend Karen Heisler. Jered and Karen had met more than a decade earlier at Live Power Community Farm (see page 41) in Mendocino County, where Jered was visiting an apprentice friend and Karen was a CSA member.

All three of them shared a dedication to CSA as a social and economic model of critical importance and had committed themselves to years of work in service to ideals they came to recognize were in large part shared. Nancy remembers, "It was the day after Jered and I got married that we talked seriously with Karen about how to pool our resources to create something that would represent the overlap of our goals." With their eye on the property that would become Pie Ranch, Jered and Nancy were eager to commit to living on and stewarding a piece of land, and Karen was prepared to

commit the necessary financial resources for the purchase. She structured an equity transfer with Jered and Nancy that valued their labor as a critical asset to the farm and created an exchange value for their labor contribution. While the trio recognized the expensive nature of land in that part of the state, it was outweighed by the value of being close to the densely populated Bay Area and Peninsula communities— critical places to raise the consciousness about the connection between urban and rural people.

FOR THE LOVE OF FAMILY FARMING

Making the transition from the university to farming and eventually child rearing has had its challenges, but Nancy equipped herself with a diverse set of skills that she learned during her years at UCSC and her time farming. She and Jered have even applied the apprenticeship model for their farm, hosting three apprentices on year-round internships.

"I love the combination of all the things that we integrate with our farm—activism, education, production," says Nancy. Nancy and Jered moved onto the farm in 2003, disked the soil, and put in their first cover crop in 2004. In 2005 they started their educational

A Model for Sustainable Farming Apprenticeships: UCSC

The University of California, Santa Cruz Apprenticeship in Ecological Horticulture began in 1967 and provides training in the concepts and practices of organic gardening and small-scale farming. Each year, thirty-five to forty-five students come to the garden to live, work, and learn. It is a working farm with a farmstand and a 125-member CSA. Community building workshops and diversity trainings teach apprentices about social issues in agriculture and support the community that forms over the six months.

The apprenticeship has developed into an internationally recognized program that blends the virtues of experiential learning with traditional classroom studies. Over six months, students take on all of the relative content of small-scale farming through their course work programming with Mission High School.

Through all of her hard work to get to where she is today, Nancy feels "grateful that Jered and I have the opportunity to share work, parenting, and Pie Ranch. We're both actively working on the farm and educational program development; and by living here on the farm we can go to a meeting for a few hours and we can share planting strawberries later. This way we both get the opportunity to raise the family and express ourselves through our professional work."

Nancy doesn't talk about money or long hours farming, but she does talk a lot about gratitude. "Seeing our children growing up on the farm and the diversity of plants and animals that comes to us is a rich exchange on the farm. This is an opportunity to connect Lucas and Rosa to farming in a new way. Kids today have no idea what food looks like in the ground and no idea that carrots don't come from bags. The very act of showing them a carrot coming out of the ground and the way they light up is truly priceless. We're excited to steward this slice of the pie and help foster a coastal corridor from San Francisco to Santa Cruz that provides organic sustainable food to the communities and engages youth in learning where their food comes from."

in soil management, composting, pest control, crop planning, irrigation, farm equipment, marketing techniques, and Community Supported Agriculture (CSA) know-how. The apprenticeship model of combining theoretical and practical instruction has been replicated both locally and internationally as apprentices go on to train others in hands-on projects. Graduates have also established their own commercial farms and market gardens, run community gardens for inner city and prison populations, and have developed school gardening programs. Many graduates take part in international development projects, including programs in Nepal, Uganda, Kenya, South Africa, and throughout Central and South America. Others have raised the standards of the organic food industry through work with certification programs and retailers.

Bringing Farms to the City: Mission Pie

While Nancy and Jered live on and steward the farm, Karen lives in her hometown of San Francisco, where she and Krystin Rubin run Mission Pie, a bakery and café that serves up sustainable foods.

Located on Mission and Twenty-Fifth Streets in a historically immigrant neighborhood, Mission Pie is surrounded by taquerías and panaderías, whose smells blend with the aromas of baking. As Karen rattles off their pies and pastries of the summer season—"Strawberry-rhubarb, peach, plum, apricot . . . "—mariachi music plays faintly from a nearby house. Behind Karen, blackboard in the café lists the local farms from which they purchase their foods. "As an urban food business," says Karen, "we want to demonstrate the mutually beneficial relationship we have with farms. This notion of 'mutual benefit' was what first turned me on about CSA, and I think there's a compelling business-to-business role to play. I'm hoping we see more of this in the coming decade—recognizing these relationships as more than just about buying local food, but actually investing in rural economies."

To help get youth more engaged, the trio recently hired a new urban-based youth programs coordinator to make the curriculum connections for high school students in sustainable food systems. And if this weren't enough, in addition to Mission Pie's commitment to buying from Pie Ranch, the business is able to contribute to growing the farm's infrastructure. The latest included equipment for grinding and milling delicious Sonoran wheat. (See more about urban farm connections in Chapter 5.)

ELIZABETH HENDERSON

FARMER,
PEACEWORK
ORGANIC FARM,
NEWARK,
NEW YORK

AUTHOR, *SHARING THE HARVEST*

People are feeling a greater need for connecting with the earth, for doing something that's positive, for taking responsibility for their lives, and ultimately, for their food," says Elizabeth Henderson. Elizabeth found true community through her work as a leader of the CSA movement, while growing food and advocating for a sustainable food system.

It was at The Putney School, a farm-orientated summer camp in Vermont, where Elizabeth found her place in the world—the combination of community, nature, and art all in one place completely enthralled her. All of the camp kids had a farm chore and hers was working in the dairy barn. "I was the assistant to the man who ran the dairy," she says, "and he took great delight in pretending to close me in every day as I would scrub out the bulk dairy vat." This early age exposure to farming and support of her activist parents for whatever she wanted to do proved a powerful combination.

Eighteen years later, Elizabeth's awareness about food, additives, and health was again heightened while raising her son. Poring over food labels, she was frightened by the fact that she couldn't pronounce most of the ingredient names. "The more labels I read, and the more ingredients that I couldn't pronounce, the more unbearable it was to feed that food to my son," she says. One smart and easy food rule of thumb is that if you can't pronounce it, it probably isn't good for you. Elizabeth came to a similar conclusion and thought, that in order to have really good food for her son—which she knew was key to his health and well-being—she would have to grow it herself. So she planted a garden.

This was a time of the burgeoning food cooperative scene, when the back-to-the-land movement was in full swing. Elizabeth and her community had a few ideas. "I got together with friends to start a college where we would educate people about sustainability, grow food, and sustain ourselves," says Elizabeth. Unfortunately, the people who worked on the concept with her were such intellectuals that they "didn't know the back end of a cow from the front end," she says. So after a stint at Boston University from 1975 to 1981, Elizabeth created a new path for herself—farming full time.

When Elizabeth headed out on her own to farm, information about how to grow food organically was hard to come by. She leaned on the intuition that she had started developing in her garden, and from her cumulative time over the years spent in Provence. In France, she experienced her first CSA and also became immersed in a culture that is world-renowned for its food traditions and small family-sized farms. The farmers grew food while not compromising the land, and in providing for their community, they lived for the revitalization of the agrarian countryside. The traditional farmers who developed CSA in France named their projects Associations pour le Maintien d'une Agriculture Paysanne (AMAP), today the country boasts over one thousand such farms.

After her first eight years as a homesteader and as a very small-scale market farmer in Massachusetts, Elizabeth moved to Rose Valley Farm in 1988, one of the first certified organic farms in the state of New York. Over the years, Elizabeth became increasingly aware of the dramatic shift in farm demographics, with imports from large farms in California and Colorado deflating food prices below what smaller farms in the northeast could produce for. She and her partners tried to think of new ways to keep the farm economically viable. Since they were located in a rural place, farmstands and farmers markets were out of the question. Those two models sometimes work, but oftentimes, many people living in rural areas either grow the same things in their gardens or purchase all of their food when they shop in town. They needed a new model.

During the cold winter months, when days were short, Elizabeth perused seed catalogs and thought about the coming year of farming. It was on one such night, that she and her business partner, David, decided that they would try a CSA. After sending out their first invitation, twenty-nine families signed up to get a share of vegetables for the year. With these members on board, Rose Valley Farm had funds for startup that spring. Each spring, farmers usually have to pay the upfront cost of producing food—the seeds, compost, fuel and other supplies that are needed to prepare beds for food production—and it's oftentimes a burden that farmers take on themselves. Unique to CSAs, members pay up front, which helps farmers early in the season (when they need it most).

Unique to the CSA model and to Elizabeth's farm, the members from the very beginning were also volunteers and would come out to the farm to harvest their vegetables. They would get their hands dirty, share in the joy of the hard work and planning, and come to the farm to be part of rural life (if only for just one day). The success of the first season led the news of the farm to travel and the farm grew to forty-five members in the succeeding year. At the end of 1990, when the farm decided that they would expand to meet the demand of one hundred members, they invited their members to help them through the growth process.

This is when the entirely uncommon association that helps run Elizabeth's farm today was formed: the Genesee Valley Organic (GVO) CSA.

Run as an unincorporated buying club, GVO CSA bought the produce from Rose Valley Farm and used their food cooperative structure to purchase other farms products such as organic wine, grape juice, strawberries, maple syrup and other things that Rose Valley didn't produce. This also allowed the farm to buffer itself from liability from having members on the farm as they helped with farm duties. This arrangement allowed the CSA to buy from other farms if Rose Valley had a bad year. It is a rare, albeit replicable, food democracy in action where the members and the farm are in full partnership.

In 1998, Elizabeth left Rose Valley when the partnership no longer worked, and moved to rented land twelve miles to the east to begin Peacework Organic Farm with her new partners, Annie and Greg Palmer. After renting the land at Peacework for a few years, the trio decided to purchase the land with the community.

The were fortunate to have an active land trust in the area that would help them with the acquisition. The Genesee Land Trust ended up buying the land and protected it from development rights. (The land is owned in perpetuity by the Land Trust and can never be developed since it is kept under an easement that designates it only be used for agricultural purposes.) The Trust then leased it back to Peacework to farm indefinitely. "Who knows, maybe it will become easier to make a living as a farmer," Elizabeth says in reference to the assistance land trusts can provide people in acquiring agricultural land. This is one of the main difficulties new farmers have when getting into farming. She also mentions that this model could become the evolution of CSA—cooperatively owned and farmed food production on "public lands," owned by non-governmental agencies such as land trusts. Since farms provide a service to the public, it makes sense that the public, the eaters of the food, should be concerned with, and proactive about, the preservation of the land on which their food grows.

As the farm transitioned, all of the great relationships and ways of sharing the workload that were established over the past ten years came too. "Having the GVO CSA worked really well." Says Elizabeth about the transition, "When the CSA couldn't get food from us in 1998 while we were getting the new property ready, they purchased food from other farms in the area."

The formal structure and procedures for the GVO CSA were developed with the help of Alison Clarke. She suggested that two people always be trained in any one job, "so that no one gets burned out saddled with a big job," says Elizabeth. They formed a team of twenty-eight core members who help keep the CSA running smoothly.

All members of the farm have a job, including a disabled woman who has been calling members every Tuesday since the CSA's inception, to remind them about their farm work shift. The workload varies depending on the size of the share, with members working two or three four-hour shifts producing food and two shifts of distribution of shares to members each year. As members get their hands dirty, they learn about the ecosystem of a farm—the soil, insects, plants, water—and its dynamic interactions with nature. It's a win-win scenario, when people with little connection to their food get reacquainted with a snap pea and the farm does not have to pay for the overhead costs of labor

In Land We Trust

Land trusts are important organizations that protect farmland from being developed. Land trusts often use conservation easements to conserve farmland. These legally binding contracts restrict the future development of the land in perpetuity. In addition to protecting the land from development, entering into a conservation easement may provide farmers with tax benefits and capital to reinvest in their agricultural operations.

Protecting farmland with any type of easement can be challenging, especially in valuable urban-edge agricultural areas that are in the path of suburban development. For example, Kathryn Lyddan, Executive Director of the Brentwood Agricultural Land Trust (BALT), in California, has found preserving the farmland in Brentwood to be politically, financially and legally complex. They have recognized that one of the most powerful tools for farmland conservation is to create a vibrant economic future for the region's farmers. BALT has been developing innovative programs to promote their farmers' products to urban residents in order to increase farmers' revenue.

Unless farming remains an economically sustainable use of the land, future generations are not as likely to take over the family farm. For aging farmers, keeping their land as farmland for future generations becomes a hard sell, especially if farm revenues are declining, their kids don't want it, and selling their land for development is the only retirement plan they have.

This is where public support of farmers and direct markets come into play. Some cities are starting to actively consider how to support local food production for their urban cores and are strategizing how to protect local farmland from development. This growing awareness of the importance of local "foodsheds" could result in urban populations supporting farmland conservation in the same way that city residents currently support open space, park, and habitat conservation.

In addition to supporting farmland conservation, we can all preserve our region's food production capacity by purchasing food direct from farmers. Progressive land trusts, such as Genesee Valley, are right there preserving the land—and in Kathryn's case, preserving and promoting the land, relationships and markets that make farming viable.

and distribution. "Farmers who do not involve the members of their CSA," says Elizabeth, "are missing the social capital, which is amazingly beneficial."

"Farmers who do not involve the members of their CSA are missing the social capital, which is amazingly beneficial."

This structure also gives Peacework freedom from the legality of having members working or volunteering on the farm. Other farms have experienced a government crackdown in the past five years for having volunteer workers and interns, as this is currently illegal—even if food, housing, or information is being traded. Because of Peacework's structure, the GVO CSA functions more like an official form of U-Pick where members pick the food that they have contracted to buy from the farm. The members are not working on the farm, but harvesting the food that they own.

Because of her knowledge of and enthusiasm for CSAs, and simply because she got asked so many questions, in 1998 Elizabeth worked to complete the first edition of *Sharing the Harvest* that was started by Robyn Van En. This book is the ultimate resource for farmers and urban folks who want to start their own CSA. Now in its second edition, the book addresses every imaginable challenge, from gender to bookkeeping to interns to land acquisition. It is an indispensable resource for anyone interested in running a CSA or a food-buying club in their community, as starting a CSA is a huge investment in administrative overhead, plant diversity, and farm infrastructure. "I hope we will be able to spread the word about community supported agriculture in language that opens doors to people. We may have to drop some of our favorite jargon—even the word 'sustainable'—and talk, instead, about keeping farms in business for the long term, making sure that everybody gets enough nourishing food to eat, and living in a way that respects the natural limits of the world around us," says Elizabeth in her book.

SPEAKING UP FOR WOMEN IN SUSTAINABLE AGRICULTURE

Beyond opening her farm to her members and creating community, Elizabeth also serves as a voice representing women in agriculture.

"I got into being a public speaker on organic agriculture twenty years ago. I was tired of the fact that Fred Kirschenmann, Wendell Berry, and Wes Jackson were the only spokespeople for sustainable agriculture since at least half of the work was, and is, being done by women." Elizabeth felt it was due time that she step up to the podium and share her view.

In addition to public speaking, Elizabeth participates in organizations that further her goals. She serves on the Board of Directors of the Northeast Organic Farming Association (NOFA) of New York, an organization with notable participation from women that promotes organic farming and information exchange about best practices. The most recent addition to her nonprofit participation is her work with a national consortium of activists dedicated to creating new standards for labor and social justice on organic and sustainably minded farms. The Agricultural Justice Project's website features a quote that sums up their work well. It's a Native American (Haudenausaunee) saying: "We need to become independent of the world market economy because the world market economy is ultimately controlled by interests which seek power or profit and which do not respond to the need of the world's peoples."[1]

When you work to create a more equitable and sustainable food system, as you do when you join a CSA or other form of buying direct from farmers, you inevitably become an activist—an activist for a new type of food system, one that does not enslave people or commodify or pollute the Earth, so that future generations too may enjoy this ethical and healthful eating.

Elizabeth is still as vibrantly passionate today about the change one can make by farming organically and involving one's community as she was when she started her journey. When asked what her advice is for present and future generations, she says, "Follow your heart. If it's what you want to do, find a way to do it. If you're alert, positive, and enjoying what you are doing, you will find a way."

DRU RIVERS

FARMER,
FULL BELLY FARM,
GUINDA,
CALIFORNIA

Full Belly Farm is a diversified organic farm with more than 1,500 CSA members and numerous other direct markets.

Full Belly Farm is one of the most beloved farms in Northern California. Just Google the name and you'll find pages upon pages of love letters, blogs, and news about farm happenings. Perhaps it's their laughing Buddha icon, but more likely it has something to do with the delicious produce they grow for over fifteen hundred people's dinner tables on a weekly basis. And that's just through their CSA.

The farm has become a destination point for city dwellers itching for a farm experience that they and their kids will invariably talk about for a lifetime. An estimated one hundred thousand people have come up the valley from all over the state, country, and world to visit since its beginnings. Passing orchard upon orchard, they make their way until they reach a large bend in the road, turn right, and then encounter 250 acres of beautiful organic farmland. Located in the apex of California's organic farming heaven, the Capay Valley boasts over sixty organic farms and was undoubtedly a large part of the reason Yolo County was "Number One Direct Marketing County in the Nation" in 2005, through sales of $8.3 million from farms direct to eaters.[2] The farm's four partners and year-round employees produce a dizzying array of edible deliciousness—citrus, stone fruits, leafy greens, solanums, nuts, honey, and wine grapes, to name a few.

Dru Rivers met Paul Muller, a fourth-generation farmer, while studying at UC Davis and serving on the advisory committee of the UC Student Farm (a working farm on the UC Davis campus that started in 1977). Dru and Paul also worked together on the Board of Directors of the Community Alliance with Family Farmers (CAFF), a nonprofit started in 1979 to support sustainable agriculture and family farmers throughout California. After finishing her undergraduate degree, Dru decided she didn't want to pursue research anymore but that she really "loved being in production agriculture," in part due to her experience on the student farm.

When Dru and Paul came upon the opportunity to buy farmland five years after they started farming the property, they weren't sure they could afford it on their own. But they realized that they didn't have to. With four partners—Dru, Paul, Judith Redmond, and Andrew Brait—they are able to share the labor, ownership, expenses, and risk inherent in farming. In this way, the Full Belly model portrays a healthy management alternative that works like a well-oiled machine. Although this arrangement requires weekly meetings, Dru is confident that bringing Judith and Andrew into the partnership has done nothing but improve their success. "I would totally not change it for the world," she says. "Working with two other partners has been so great and it's sometimes hard, but I would say 99.9 percent of the time we get along so well and make great decisions together, and we all complement each other," she says. This model also allows the partners more of an opportunity to have a life outside of the farm.

"What is so real and inspiring to me is the day-to-day, people getting their hands dirty and discovering that they love farming."

Not that the partners have much extra time. Paul serves as the Capay Valley Vision board president; Dru has been on the Ecological Farming Association board for twenty-two years; and Judith has served in various capacities of the Community Alliance with Family Farmers. They are all active in their communities in addition to being in charge of a particular crop.

For Dru, this means she's in charge of the two hundred sheep raised for meat and yarn and three hundred quibbling hens that lay eggs for the house and the CSA. She keeps the milk flowing with the farm's goats (mostly for cheese), and that of the five dairy cows (just for the farm's use). She is also in charge of the crop that spreads a smile over everyone's face at their weekly farmers markets and the one that landed her a *National Geographic* feature—flowers. Big, beautiful bouquets of poppies, sunflowers, Dutch iris, bachelor buttons, snapdragons, and whatever is in season for both fresh and dried arrangements.

The division of labor worked out well for her. "If I had to choose," she says, "I would choose these two—animals and flowers—because they keep me really happy."

THINKING INSIDE THE BOX

CSA farms like Full Belly have taken the wholesale produce box that contains just one item and have filled it with seasonal splendor. Full Belly jumped into the box in 1995 with an initial fifty CSA customers. While CSA models and product offerings are as variable as the farms themselves, they stick to a general rule of keeping it simple. "We only have one size of box. We don't let people choose what goes in their box; it's whatever we decide. And still, people just love it," says Dru. "And we get so much great feedback. Every week we get love letter after love letter after love letter."

The farm delivers to twenty-five sites in eight cities around the Bay Area and has pickups at farmers markets, which helps bring more people to the markets. Members do have a say in the frequency of their delivery and can add on special seasonal items, like carrots for juicing, lamb (meat, wool, hides), fresh-cut flowers, stoneground whole wheat, walnuts and almonds, etc. The exhaustive list would be, well, exhausting.

As a CSA member, getting into the box requires a mental shift in terms of how you plan and prepare your meals. Your cookbooks and the Internet will become your greatest kitchen friends for identifying and finding new ways to prepare all the seasonal ingredients. This model makes it possible to move away from the global availabilities of our conventional supermarkets and into sustainable, more environmentally savvy agriculture products. Even the most intrepid cook, who might feel overwhelmed at having to create a chard menu for eight weeks (one of the most common member complaints), will delight in being more connected to the seasons—variety and abundance clearly varying depending on location in the U.S.

Because Full Belly is located in California, they are able to grow seasonal food year-round. (Colder weather areas can grow year round too, if they use greenhouses and hoop houses—technologies that are starting to become more widespread and energy efficient.) In winter there are greens, roots, persimmons, grapefruit, lemons, pomegranates, and oranges. Summer brings the bounty of melons, tomatoes, eggplant, peppers, corn, beans, herbs, and more. Full Belly Farm grows 150 varieties of fruits, vegetables, nuts, and some really fun new foods like popcorn, beans, flours and almond butter.

At Full Belly, every week of the year represents the changing seasons with eight or nine different items. The summer box is completely different from the winter box, and there are all those nuances in between, with decadent varieties coming in and out of season all the time. There's always a new surprise.

GROWING THE FUTURE THROUGH TRAINING THE NEXT GENERATION

Dru and the farm offer internship opportunities where people can come to the farm and learn all about organic agriculture. By bringing new faces out to the farm, the internship program has undoubtedly helped proliferate knowledge of organic and diversified growing practices. While it requires a whole slew of considerations—housing, legality, insurance, etc.—both the farm and society benefit from farmers' willingness to educate and train the next generation through hands-on learning.

Dru and her partners know that it requires substantial work on their end but believe that training future generations of farmers is inherently important. They offer four on-farm internships that last for a full year. Since they started their intern program, the farm has had over one hundred interns. Dru proudly reports that around thirty have gone on to start their own farms. Women are showing up more frequently to learn too. Dru says they get a ten-to-one ratio of women to men applying to work there. "I know all of these women who have left here and who are going on to farm. That's what is so real and inspiring to me—the day-to-day, people getting their hands dirty and discovering that they love it. They love their hands getting callused. It's so fun for me to see it and to watch women go through that and know that they are really capable." She gets excited by the fact that so many women come out to the farm to learn, grow, and test their skills at growing food and speaks extensively on the subject of women and farming at various state and national conferences.

Despite the aging demographic of farmers in our country, Full Belly Farm has seen nothing but an increase in people interested in coming to the farm to work, learn and experience what their lifestyle has to offer.

They also host a variety of farm tours throughout the year and bring classes and groups of kids to the farm to get down and dirty with farming. While farmers should have a goal to earn some money from visits that require their time and planning, Dru remarks that it probably doesn't bring in very much money, but "it sure makes us a lot of friends!" The farm has hosted visits with kids for the past twenty years and hosts about three hundred school kids per year. "They love the animals," says Dru. "That's always the first thing they want to see." The students sometimes stay overnight as well. "It's so important, because for some of these kids it will be the only time in their whole lives that they'll ever spend a night on the farm. And actually, for many parents this is also true. It's really about educating the parents and the kids," she says.

> "Most people don't know that land equals food and farmers equal food, and it's really important to raise people's consciousness up to that level."

Dru and her partners see the impact this experience has on the kids as some of them have grown and have applied for internships. "The first time it happened it was so cool. We got this letter saying, 'I came to your farm in the third grade and it made the biggest impression on me for my whole life. I'm looking for farm work and I want to come and learn how to work on your farm.' It's coming full circle; a lot of those kids came here for a brief moment in their lives, but I'm sure they carry it around with them and it affects their decisions—where to live, how to live their lives, whatever values that we might have instilled in them now they're of voting age. It's so neat to know that it does impact so many people."

HOES DOWN: A COMMUNITY HARVEST CELEBRATION

Fall is in the air—the farm is full of music, food, laughter, and thousands of people. While farming is pretty much year round in California, October definitely marks a less intensive season than spring and summer during which farmers are logging eighty-hour weeks in the rush and bustle to get ripening food to people's plates. There's really nothing like a harvest celebration. At Full Belly Farm, Hoes Down is an annual event that celebrates the year's bountiful harvest and the time for the farm to put their hoes to rest.

"This past year was the biggest," says Dru, who is on the planning committee every year. "About five thousand people came out, mostly from the Bay Area." When asked about the profits from the event, she says with a smile, "We donate the majority of it to a few nonprofits." In addition to music, dancing, and great organic food, beer and wine, there's a kids area organized by Annie Main of Good Humus Farm (a neighbor in the valley) with apple bobbing, a dunk tank, a straw-bale maze (created by Annie's son Zach), storytelling, crafts, sheep shearing, cow milking—you get the idea. It's the best on-farm festival many will ever experience. Camping is allowed overnight and the youngsters on the farm stay up late playing music down by Cache Creek, which runs along the edge of the farm. The second day is full of workshops at neighboring farms for attendees that stay over to get their questions answered about chickens, bees, biofuels, and other farm-related topics.

Dru believes that the connection for city people, getting to come out and feel the land, is as much a part of their work as growing gorgeous food. It's a way to show the importance of the farm through the hands-on experience of being there. "It's so important for us to have a day when we have people here just learning about what we are doing and having the transparency between the farm and the people that buy our food. People realize, 'Wow, this is where my food comes from and I want to support this no matter what happens. I'll vote in favor of this farm, this farmland, this valley.' Many people don't know that land equals food and farmers equal food, and it's really important to raise people's consciousness up to that level."

THE CHOICE TO STAY SMALL

Over the years, Full Belly has become a very successful family business and organic farm—so successful, in fact, that Dru and her partners often get requests to sell at more markets and to grow their business. Being pressured to produce more food is a good problem for a farm to have, in some ways. This question of scale—what is truly a sustainable sized farm that can meet market demand and grow diversely?—often comes up with the partners during their meetings. "Scale is always an issue," says Dru. "Are we too big? Could we get bigger? Do we want to? These are tough questions." The size of the farm, considered large by other states' sustainable farm standards and medium-sized for California, generally determines the number of crops you grow. Dru points out that the larger a farm gets, the more removed the farmer gets from what's growing, what's happening, and how they are connected to the day-to-day.

So for now, the partners at Full Belly Farm plan to stick with their 250 acres and focus on growing better quality foods on the land they already have. Most important of all for Dru and her partners: keeping farming exciting.

"There are so many fun things to think about doing, and it makes our kids want to come back and farm with us because it's fun and exciting. That's how it has to be because it's a lot of friggin' work. If it's not exciting, then farmers get bored. That's why a lot of kids left the farm fifty years ago, because they thought it was really boring to plant one thousand acres of wheat."

> The larger a farm gets, the more removed the farmer gets from what's growing, what's happening, and how they are connected to the day-to-day.

The True Cost of Food

When asked the question of whether people are willing to pay the "true cost of food," Dru answers, "I feel that the people are willing to make a fair exchange for what we bring to the farmers market. It's tricky—in some places it's a little harder for people to swallow the true cost of food. The current economic situation makes it hard." This cost is the real monetary value that is required to produce food that is free of pesticides, that pays a fair working wage to farmers and farm workers, and that produces food on the land with future generations in mind. What we see in conventional grocery stores hardly reflects conventional food production, whose "negative externalities" of excessive water use, soil erosion, pollution via shipping and chemical application are not equated for.

But, says Dru, "I feel that organic farmers, or at least the ones that I know, are more gutsy at trying to get a real cost for their food." This cost is complex, considering the amount of inputs that go into growing, say, a tomato. Those who practice sustainable agriculture have additional costs that increase the price—crop diversity, labor, and organic certified treatments and the certification itself are more expensive than conventional means of production at this point in time. Sustainability-minded farmers do not grow mono-crops (plantings of one type), and they do not uniformly apply massive amounts of pesticides or herbicides. Truly sustainable farms have mixed plantings with various types of fruits and vegetables to avoid losing entire crops to a fungus or insect. Diversity happens to be an insurance policy of sorts in the natural world. For this reason, smaller farms (less than five hundred acres) use more hand labor and less machinery, which also increases the price.

"I still see conventional growers selling green beans for $1 a pound, and there is no way we can grow green beans for that price," says Dru exasperatedly. "We hand pick, hand wash, and truck it all to the market. I think all farmers—organic and conventional—need to get more realistic about paying workers a fair wage (one of the reasons prices are artificially low), and ask more money for their food so workers can get paid more fairly."

EMILY OAKLEY

FARMER, THREE
SPRINGS FARM,
OAKS, OKLAHOMA

Three Springs is a full-
time organic vegetable
farm with a CSA program.

When spring comes, Emily Oakley mulches blueberries nonstop—something she would never have done without her learned experiences in Providence, Rhode Island, and at Full Belly Farm in California as an intern. After finishing her year of organic farm boot camp at Full Belly, she pursued her master's degree at the University of California Davis.

While it is easier to live near people that share your views and opinions, it's good to spread the gospel of radical thinking, in this case that of sustainable agriculture, into new parts of the country. Emily and her partner, Mike, loved farming in California, but they decided to start their own farm in Emily's hometown of Tulsa, Oklahoma, in 2003.

Full Belly and other farms in Northern California can benefit from their close proximity to the affluent foodie crowd of the Bay Area and year-round production, but Tulsa is a different gastronomic beast. Emily points out that "as with any metropolitan area, there are foodies in Tulsa, but in describing the cuisine around here, most people would probably name barbecue, fried chicken, and potato salad as typical. We've found that offering recipes for unusual crops has helped us sell many new veggies to our customers, like mizuna or purple potatoes."

According to Emily, the state has more cattle and meat animals than humans, with farms near Three Springs consisting of cattle ranches and Tyson chicken farms. You can see the birds stacked on semi trucks, in crate upon crate, headed down the highway towards the processing plants. Once processed, the chicken isn't even sent to local stores, but rather travels long distances for redistribution. While Oklahoma's landscape is changing (dotted with some vegetables), it's still mostly (non-organic) meat—a huge environmental offender. (Conventional meat uses exorbitant water; trucking; is corn intensive, which embodies yet another trail of pollution; and contributes meth-ane—a greenhouse gas—to the atmosphere.)

But down the road, Three Springs has created a different reality. Of the twenty acres Emily owns with Mike, three and a half are diversely cultivated in mixed annual vegetables and herbs,

"Eating habits can evolve into more sustainable living habits."

and one and a half acres are divided among blueberries, asparagus, and apples. The rest they have used to conserve wildlife habitat by planting native species and hedgerows—plantings that provide homes for wildlife and pollinators while blocking wind (which is destructive to many annual food crops). She and Mike try to grow everything in order to learn what their land will and will not grow. "We definitely do not grow parsnips!" she says of the failed crop, proving that "trial and error" is definitely a legitimate research technique.

At the local farmers market, Emily represents the sole full-time organic vegetable farm in the market. "There are a lot of hobbyists and people that have taken it on as a part-time income, to supplement their retirement or otherwise—but no one is doing organic vegetable farming full-time like we are," she says. "I would give up the lack of competition to have a true farming community in a minute." (The 2007 Agricultural Census says that the highest concentration of organic farms are considered "hobby" or "retired," folks whose annual sales amount to less than $10,000.[3])

What is truly invigorating for her has been the broad-based community support. "Every year I almost start crying from happiness because we've achieved so many relationships. What keeps me going is the human element with what we do," she says. "Someone out there is going to eat the food we grow; it will be someone's dinner and we know that person. I'm so lucky to do it and we're so lucky that we have them. They are really good customers."

AN INNOVATOR OF CSA: PICK YOUR OWN BOX

In her first year, Emily sold at the local farmers market and started a CSA with ten friends and family members. "Mike and I wanted to start small so that we wouldn't owe people a lot of money, and if something went wrong, well, our friends and family would be more forgiving," she says. Finding a lot of her old community ties still intact proved invaluable to the CSA's successful start. To date, no marketing has been necessary—the farm has used good old-fashioned word of mouth and an information table at the farmers market to get new members. Now, they have a waiting list and more members than they can accommodate each year.

They also have a really unique CSA model, one that doesn't include the traditional "box." "We let our members pick out what they want at the farmers market," says Emily. "There are pluses and minuses, for sure. For example, if you get to the market late, your pickings won't be very good. But members know to arrive on the earlier side so they have a diversity of stuff to pick from. This way we don't have to worry about packing boxes, and people get to pick out what they truly want." This method of putting the responsibility on their members helps Emily and Mike minimize the labor for their CSA. It's a truly innovative model that reduces the farm's overhead costs and brings people to the market.

FARMING AND SOCIAL JUSTICE

Emily's interest in growing food evolved from her intrigue with good environmental stewardship but also through the realm of labor issues involved in the production of food as well. "I started learning more about social justice, and came to farming thinking that farmers were the bad guys and sustainable agriculture was a solution, the answer to our ills. I've learned that it's so much more complicated than that," she says. The farming system includes environmental elements such as land, water and diversity, but it also involves eaters. Many people assume they contribute to positive social justice when they buy organic or local, but from Emily's perspective, this is not always the case. As organic food and smaller producers are forced to be price competitive in the global economy and by the nature of diversified food production, they require more hand laborers. Because of this, Emily and Mike have decided that they aren't going to hire any workers unless they can afford to pay them a living wage. "People in California told us that it wasn't possible to make enough money farming with two people, but it is possible here," she says. To date, they still don't have any paid employees, but they are managing just fine.

On top of her full-time farming, managing the CSA, and running the stand at the Tulsa farmers market, Emily also serves as the vice president of operations for the market, where she has worked to increase the accessibility of the market. For example, the market accepts the Women, Infants and Children program (WIC) and the market has just purchased the machine to accept food stamps so that low-income folks can access fresh fruits and vegetables.

TAKING ADVANTAGE OF GENDER DIFFERENCES

Talking of their farmers market stand, Emily openly admits that while she doesn't want to believe that gender division of labor happens, there are definitely roles she and Mike take on based on gender. For example, Emily brings administration, communication, and marketing skills, along with a friendly smile. "It's such a stereotype," she says knowingly. "But there are many truths, such as, if we send Mike to the market alone, we sell less. You have to smile, be approachable and friendly. Marketing is something that I feel comfortable with."

In addition to her welcoming graces, the CSA newsletter is something that she produces. She knows that Mike can do it as well, but feels she adds a certain pizzazz and magic in the telling of what's happening on the farm that is lost in Mike's translation. "He approaches the newsletter more earnestly," she says, "as he may be more straightforward about the details of the farm and less focused on telling the story well." And, according to Emily, the way that women think about and handle the physicality of farming also varies from the approach of men. "Mike tries to work through problems with his physical strength and will look for an implement to use, while I try to think about how I can get it done without a machine. I think men love equipment, and while women like equipment too, it's a different relationship," she says.

FARM SMARTER, NOT HARDER

While the two might differ in their marketing appeal, storytelling, and problem-solving mechanics, one thing that they both agree on is money. It was a little shocking to hear Emily say, "Last year we decided we were going to work less, and we ended up making more money"—an oxymoronic statement in the farming business. She and Mike are always looking for more ways to be an efficient two-person operation. "We decided to go to market for twenty-one weeks [versus the previous longer season] and made more than the previous year." Here's how they did it. The two sat down and did the math, deciding how much money they wanted to make to provide for their needs. Emily acknowledges that they have a simple lifestyle—they don't go out to eat every week and don't buy new things very often. After they determined their financial benchmark, they made an agreement that they wouldn't work more than they needed to. She's convinced that they will generate more profit by farming smarter, not more, with their goal to decrease their acreage every year until they reach that happy place where scale and savings meet.

They have even decided not to bring interns or apprentices on the farm—a way to have a work/knowledge exchange that typically benefits a farm's labor capacity. Despite the lure of having interns or apprentices, Emily has found that they don't fit in well with what she wants to do, saying, "I can't farm the way I want to while having someone else that I have to mentor—it's a big commitment." Instead of interns, she hosts numerous tours each year for students, prospective farmers from other countries, and customers, such as the farmer from Nigeria who was on the farm recently for a cultural and farming exchange. As avid travelers, both she and Mike love to learn about international agricultural issues, an activity that is supported by the seasonal nature of their farm, not a luxury not afforded in states that grow year round.

Despite all of their success, it hasn't always been easy in Oklahoma. Emily keeps trying to lure friends to come to visit by saying "Tulsa is the new Portland," and is a little dismayed that it hasn't caught on yet. Regardless, she and Mike are as happy as blueberries, living their purpose and building a more robust local food economy for their community. Emily feels that food "is a really good place for people to start taking responsibility for their lives. If you start thinking about the story behind a plate of food, who knows where you'll go from there? Eating habits," she says, "can evolve into more sustainable living habits."

GLORIA DECATER

FARMER,
LIVE POWER
COMMUNITY FARM,
COVELO,
CALIFORNIA

Live Power is a 40-acre
biodynamic/organic
CSA farm that provides
fresh, high-quality
food for 200 people.

Small, organic family farmers really can feed the world. While this has been demonstrated for centuries by indigenous peoples of the world, and reported by the Food and Agriculture Organization of the United Nations, ecological—small, sustainable and organic—farming is debunking the myth that has predominated our agriculture system in the United States for the last one hundred years: that chemicals and mechanized means are necessary to feed our growing population.[4] Live Power Farm, the oldest CSA in the state of California, is backing up these beliefs by feeding two hundred families on a mere forty-acre land base. Gloria Decater and her husband, Stephen, think of the farm as a whole operating system and measure their productivity differently. They incorporate fertility and energy produced on farm in their equation of success. No truckloads of nitrogen here—they compost their animal waste, use solar, capture rainwater, and are almost an entirely closed energy loop, producing what they need on the farm through smart management of resources. For the farm's CSA members in San Francisco/Bay Area and Mendocino County, being involved in the farm means more than just buying potatoes, fruits and vegetables; it also means taking care of the land and the people who grow their food in a truly regenerative way.

By partnering with a handful of other farms, Gloria and Stephen offer their members a full-meal-deal year-round, which includes the vegetable crops from Live Power as well as a variety of organic and biodynamically grown fruits, eggs, meats, flowers, and rice, all produced on farms within a two-hundred-mile radius of the Decaters' home.

Gloria's story in farming started in the 1970s when she moved out to California from New Jersey to attend a Waldorf teacher training school in Los Angeles. With her heart in nature and education, Gloria was drawn north to Covelo, California, where Alan Chadwick, a legendary teacher of organic farming and gardening, held an apprenticeship program. Chadwick is the original founder of the University of California Santa Cruz's Center for Agroecology, which runs the Farm and Garden Apprenticeship program well known for hands-on, interactive training.

Needless to say, Gloria never left Covelo—it's where she happened to meet Stephen as he was working as Chadwick's assistant. The two instantly fell for each other with their shared vision for sustainable food and farming, while they learned extensively about biodynamic agriculture.

FARMING WITH THE COSMOS: BIODYNAMICS

The rich soil, hearty vegetables, happy animals and satisfied CSA members of Live Power are in a large part due to the biodynamic practices that increase soil fertility on the Decaters' farm. Biodynamic farming works with microbes in the soil to produce bountiful harvests through supporting, harmonizing with, and enhancing natural processes and life forces. The Demeter Association, the organizing body that certifies biodynamic producers, says that biodynamic farming includes the cosmic and planetary rhythms of the earth in its ecological approach. These practices take into account planetary and star constellation alignments that can be utilized to create harmony between soil activity and plant growth. And this isn't just happening in California—Demeter certifies producers for their biodynamic processes worldwide. Farmers that use such practices all witness an astounding return of soil vitality. Even if you're not a believer in biodynamics and its connection to cosmic events, there's something about it that truly brings greater quality and balanced productivity on a farm. This increased fertility has been tested and evaluated by the Demeter Association on farms they certify the world over.[5]

According to Gloria, "Biodynamic preparations stimulate humus formation and help improve soil development and texture, making it more receptive and responsive to [the aforementioned] earthly and cosmic life forces and processes." Preparations of plant material, manure or quartz meal are placed in the organ of an animal (usually a horn or stomach) and are buried and fermented for at least six months on a particular calendar date. After the preparations are ready, they are applied on both vegetative matter (vegetables, fruit orchards, etc.) as well as compost to increase the biological connection and fertility of the farm.

The Decaters immediately saw the difference in the soil after they started using the Demeter-approved applications on their compost. In addition to greater soil fertility, they have noticed an increase in water retention—an essential component that ensures plants can better survive water shortages while simultaneously strengthening their roots.

Even the process of applying the preparations is beneficial to the soil as it stimulates the top layer of humus and organic matter. The preps also attract beneficial microorganisms, insects and worms that make soil healthy. With each teaspoon said to be home to millions of creatures, the interrelationships between the soil and our food still holds mysteries for farmers and scientists alike. What we do know is that "live" soil is a very good thing. But worms and water are only part of a healthy farm system. As Gloria points out, what they have implemented, and what we need more of in this country, is a reduction of the farm's pollution footprint. "A farm's external inputs often include tillage and water pumping energy, animal feed, and fertility materials. All of these things can be generated on the farm to make it an incredible, whole organism," says Gloria.

Having a diversity of plants and animals fosters amazing cycles of mutual support within the organism of the farm. The plant material, fed to the animals, comes back to the soil as manure and compost. This enables the soil to produce food for animals, people, and soil organisms.

Doing an awful lot on just forty acres, the Decaters cultivate only four acres of vegetables to feed their family and 200 CSA members. The animals rotate around the two- to four-acre fields, as does the vegetable garden, moving every five years or so. Gloria and Stephen's mantra of the "farm as an ecosystem" has helped to grow beautiful things, including a tight-knit circle of eaters fully committed to the farm's wellbeing.

SOLAR POWER AND DRAFT HORSES

"Watching and listening to a team of horses in the field," Gloria muses, "is totally different than working with a tractor. I'm watching Stephen in the garden right now, and those Belgian amber horses against the green are so beautiful and perfect. They are living beings with character and personality." The Belgians the Decaters rely on instead of tractors are bred specifically for heavy work, live for many years, and have the strength and speed to get a lot of work done. She also points out how self-sufficient the horses are since they are "solar based": they eat feed that is grown with the energy of the sun right on the farm. They are off-grid and they don't cause soil erosion when worked with carefully. If you've ever seen a tractor in the field, you notice the swirl of dirt flying around, that's the topsoil—the most precious six-inch layer of soil we have that largely determines soil fertility. But with the horses, there is hardly dust. If that weren't reason enough to use horses, Gloria notes how little soil compaction there is when you don't have a tractor running over the soil (compaction decreases fertility and water absorption).

Besides using the sun to produce feed for the animals that incidentally both work on the farm and produce manure fertilizer, the Decaters also harvest the sunlight energy for their electrical needs and pumping water. They're tied into the electrical grid, so their meter goes backwards during the sunniest parts of the year, when they earn credit that then gets used during cloudier times. They produce about 70 percent of their energy needs via solar panels, which they were able to acquire and install due to the rebates offered by the California Energy Commission. They plan to install solar thermal panels for their hot water system, which will get them closer to 90 percent. And just in case the grid ever goes down, they have a battery pack, since they would need to operate water pumps for the animals and circuits for the office and house. The farm brings a new level to the word "self-sufficient." If even half of our remaining 3.3 million farmers grew food for 200 families each, like the Decaters, we would have more than enough food for our 308 million–plus citizens, even if we had to adjust what "local" means.

IT TAKES A COMMUNITY TO SUPPORT A FARM

It takes a farm to feed a community, and it takes a community to support that farm. As stalwarts of "beyond organic" farming practices and direct farm-to-community relationships since the beginning, Gloria and Stephen remain firmly grounded in the belief that "relationship based" farming has great impact on the present and future viability of family farms in the United States. Gloria gets really excited when she talks about what a huge difference it makes to the economic stability and security of the farm when there is a community of dedicated members standing behind the farm rather than support of the farm being left completely at the mercy of fluctuations and chance in the marketplace.

Gloria's original plan after leaving the Waldorf training program was to start a farm school. Live Power Community Farm is thirty-five years old, and after ten years of establishing the farm with Stephen, Gloria was able to begin creating the Farm School Program of her dreams. For twenty-five years, school classes have been coming to the farm from the Bay Area and locally, about ten visits each year for school classes grades 3 through 10. The children, teachers, and parents stay on the farm for three days and nights and learn the rhythms and tasks of taking care of the soil, plants, animals, and infrastructure of the farm. "What I see as important is that the kids learn how to think and work hard. I believe that has a lot to do with carrying responsibilities and solving practical problems while living and working on a farm. Invariably it's a great experience for all of the children but a powerful one for all of the parents as well. I've had many people in tears when they are leaving, saying 'Oh, okay, this is what's important, what we need to work together to create.' "

The Decaters work with five to seven apprentice farmers each year, too, with many sticking around for multiple seasons because there's so much to learn.

"Our focus is to educate and support people to go back into farming—that's how we should be creating community," says Gloria. "Education, education, education, provided by opportunities to have people on the farm and to have a relationship to the farm. I get so many emails from members saying, 'I'm so glad you informed us that the farm experienced frost, so I know why there are no tomatoes!' It brings them so much closer; they are protecting and supporting this place."

"Our focus is to educate and support people to go back into farming."

Gloria is enlivened by conversations about organic farming; and by virtue of having CSA and member workdays, she sees the difference that connecting with the soil makes for people. "It not only saves your stomach but it saves your soul; it brings people together. People feel so great doing the work. When you see that soil turn over and see the fertility and realize that generation after generation of people, for ten thousand years, have done that work—composting, plowing, building soil, devoting their lives to caring for the earth—then you feel a connection to the past and the future. Visitors get a little tired after a couple of trips down the furrow, saying 'Whoa, those horses are strong!' They are in awe! The soil is being opened and they are feeling, smelling, and seeing it."

Both Gloria and Stephen have been acknowledged for their contributions to sustainable agriculture by the CSA movement and organic and biodynamic farming community. They are a continuing inspiration to Mendocino County and San Francisco community members that enjoy their foods. Gloria, in turn, is inspired by all of the people and knows that so many kids have grown up on their food and that throughout their lives they will be on the lookout for a CSA near them. "Everyone needs to eat," says Gloria, "but we also need to be more connected to and supportive of the land and people that grow the food. Food and farming are the basis of our culture."

RECIPES FOR ACTION

Farmers markets, CSAs and other alternative ways of selling and growing food are rebuilding the historic ties between producers and their urban counterparts. Here are some ideas for getting involved (see also the Resources section of the book).

EATER

As an eater, your food dollar determines what size farms we will have—small, medium, or gigantic; local and organic or conventional and industrial. Here's how you can support sustainable food and farming by voting with your fork:

• **Join a CSA.**
You can find one near you by going to www.eatwellguide.org or www.localharvest.org.

• **Start with a small commitment and grow it.**
If you don't shop at a farmers market regularly, try going once a month. Pick a particular day, such as the third Saturday or Sunday of the month. If that suits you, try increasing that to once a week for your fresh (and some prepared) foods. You'll notice the difference in flavor, and if you buy at the peak of the season prices, will be comparable to the supermarket. Farmers get a greater percentage of your dollar when you buy direct.

• **Shop at your locally owned natural food store or even better, a member or worker-owned food co-op (if you don't have one, see next step).**

• **Start a food-buying club.**
If you're ready to get some great prices on organic food and build community at the same time, consider starting a neighborhood buying club or food co-op. Neighborhood food-buying clubs offer members the opportunity to purchase food in bulk from farmers markets

and wholesalers. Members also avoid supermarket retail markups and reduce packaging by buying in bulk. Consider partnering with a farm or many farms for fresh product. See The Park Slope Food Coop, www .foodcoop.com, and The Cog, www.thecog.org, for examples.

- **Encourage more local foods wherever you eat or shop.**
- Talk to a manager, or leave a comment in the suggestion box. If you're at a restaurant, leave a comment with your bill if you don't want to ask your waiter.
- Ask grocers and restaurants to identify the farms and/or county of origin for the food they sell.
- Learn about food seasons in your area so that you'll know more about what is and what isn't locally grown. Ask farmers at the market or do some research on your own. See www.epicurious.com/ articlesguides/seasonalcooking/farmtotable/seasonalingredientmap for an example.

- **Help those in need.**

If you want to get involved for the cause of others who don't have access to fresh fruits and vegetables, consider volunteering at your local food pantry/bank, helping out at your local Food Not Bombs chapter, or getting your church, sports group, or whatever civic group you're part of, involved.

- Food Not Bombs—a group formed out of the antiwar movement that is dedicated to feeding people for free. To find a chapter in your area or for a step-by-step guide to creating a chapter, visit www .foodnotbombs.net.
- Food Banks—provide emergency food for people who need it. Some also have gardens. Visit Feeding America's website to find a food bank near you and donate or volunteer. Encourage your local food bank or church to start an organic food garden. www.feedingamerica.org
- SNAP (Supplemental Nutrition Assistance Program, formerly called Food Stamps). Advocate that your local farmers' market and CSA accept SNAP. For more information on SNAP and eligibility visit www.fns.usda.gov/FSP/.

- The Ecology Center spearheaded the movement for farmers' markets in California to accept EBT. Some of their resources are California specific, but many are applicable across the country. See www.ecologycenter.org/ebt.

• Can and preserve foods.
Canning and preserving foods is economical and preserves the flavors of the seasons. You can buy bulk when fruits and vegetables are at their peak and are the least expensive. And do not be afraid! People have been canning, jamming and fermenting for centuries. As long as you follow safety instructions, your odds of getting food poisoning are very low.

FARMER

As a producer of food, here are some ways to get food direct to your community.

• Start a CSA. Everything you need to know is in *Sharing the Harvest*. (See Bibliography.)

• Sell direct to food businesses.
(Adapted from UC SAREP's "Selling Directly to Restaurants and Retailers")
- Research your audience, always a good rule of thumb before going to meet with someone. Check out the business's website or see what you can find through an online search.
- Eat or shop at the business prior to discussing selling to it to become more familiar with its customer base and angle.
- Get your story straight. Bring brochures, business cards, and a list of availabilities and prices.
- Bring samples! At retailers it may also be possible to offer free samples to customers.
- Know what price you need for your products.
- Know your seasonality and the amounts of product you'll have available. Keep store and/or restaurant managers aware of any

changes in your production. Focus on being consistent, reliable, punctual and clear, not only with deliveries but also with billing and updates on availability. Let them know how often you can deliver and how often you will send availabilities (via fax or email). Get the name of the appropriate person to follow up with.

- Compile a list of potential new vendors and have a farm day for businesses. Bring them out to the farm to sample your products.
- Market yourself through your website and by getting listed on Localharvest.org, Eatwellguide.org, and on local sites such as regional Buy Fresh Buy Local (active in forty states) chapters.
- If Slow Food is active in your area, partner up on an event.

• Sell at your local farmers market.

Farmers markets are great places to get the word out about your farm. Many farms start at markets, establish their CSAs and direct markets, and eventually opt out to open the door for others. Many markets have wait lists these days, so plan to get on the wait lists early or consider starting a new market (a BIG endeavor that can be managed with a group).

• Bring eaters onto your farm.

While not every farm is set up for this or wants to do it, open houses on your farm build a stronger connection to your eaters, and you can get work done! You never know who might show up—chefs, journalists, retailers—that will prove to be a friend of the farm.

- Consider requiring an RSVP so you know how many people to expect.
- Charge a fee to cover your costs of time and any print material you may need to promote the event and to create signs to keep people from stepping on your beds.
- Liability insurance is a must.

FOOD BUSINESS

As a business, you can show your community support by buying and serving locally grown foods. Your vendors (i.e. farmers) and customers will thank you. Here are a few ways that businesses can support family farmers and encourage sustainable food production:

• **Buy direct from farmers.**
• Make connections through your farmers market or contact your agricultural extension office for suggestions. You can find this by going to your county agriculture department's home page.
• Search for local farmers at Localharvest.org, Eatwellguide.org, or your local Slow Food or Buy Fresh Buy Local chapter.
• Things to consider if wanting to buy more locally grown foods: storage (farmers usually can only deliver one to two times per week), availability changes with seasonality, marketing/messaging for your customers, increases in invoicing.
• Ask your current distributor for transparency (farm identification) and let them know that you prefer locally grown foods.

• **Host a CSA drop site.**
Serving as a site for a local farmer to drop off weekly CSA shares will connect you not only to a local farmer, but also with the farm's eaters who love local food. It may seem counterintuitive, but it will draw new people to your store and increase your sale of value-added products and other food items. Check out www.csacenter.org for more information.

• **For restaurants: Highlight in-season foods.**
Changing your menu with the seasons allows you to take advantage of great seasonal flavor and, many times, great prices. Celebrate the arrival of asparagus, tomatoes, butternut squash or just the coming of a new season with a special meal. Tell your customers about your sourcing practices. They will thank you.

CHAPTER 2

ADVOCATES FOR SOCIAL CHANGE

G ardening in your backyard and shopping at your farmers market are two great ways to start to supporting sustainable agriculture. But above and beyond these important daily acts, we need to advocate for reform on how our billions of tax dollars are spent on subsidizing food and farming in the United States. Currently they are mostly supporting industrial agriculture over more sustainable practices, but the women in this chapter—media-makers, researchers, organizers, writers, and political gurus—are educating and advocating for reform to help change the way America eats and farms.

Policy and media—where the rubber meets the road—is key to getting the government and our tax dollars aligned with our values of sustainability. And because we are so influenced by media, be it radio, TV, or the web, it has become one of our most critical allies in changing policy. Perhaps never before could advocates mobilize people so quickly about issues. The web, blogs, social networking sites, and email are a few of the myriad ways that people are getting information. While these tools aren't covered exclusively by any one woman in this chapter, each of them certainly uses them to get the word out about their advocacy. The innovative use of digital technology, found in The Meatrix, for example, proves that the web can be used for the betterment of our food system. To date, twenty million people worldwide have viewed the animated shorts that illustrate the absurdity, cruelty, and food contamination common on today's factory farms. The Grace Foundation, which produced the series, also manages the Eat Well Guide, a website with thousands of listings for sources of fresh local meat, dairy, and produce throughout North America. Eat Well director Destin Joy Layne says, "The demand for this information is huge and continues to grow." And because we can communicate more quickly, effectively, and in most cases, more cheaply, through today's media, all of us can become more politically active and stay up-to-date with the issues and legislation that are impacting what we eat.

A more informed public takes action and creates the vim for political change by writing letters and calling representatives. New bills are written, and the public must again put the pressure on legislators to ensure that funding is allocated to support the legislation. This is how we can get more funding for organic farming research, assistance for farmers wanting to transition from conventional to organic, resources for schools to incorporate local foods and gardens, and funding for conservation programs on farms. Every one of our tax dollars that supports sustainable food, communities, and the environment gets us one step closer to a food system that does not compromise the environment or people's health.

As the women in this chapter will tell you, what type of food that is served for dinner is really up to you and me, and what gets us started is their work as storytellers, advocates, and bridge builders.

CLAIRE HOPE CUMMINGS

LAWYER AND INDIGENOUS LAND RIGHTS ADVOCATE

AUTHOR, *UNCERTAIN PERIL: GENETIC ENGINEERING AND THE FUTURE OF SEEDS*

At the heart of sustainable farming and food production is a feminine energy of fertility, rebirth, and nurturing. It is this regenerative power that is inspiring the process of social change," says Claire Hope Cummings. Her lifetime of advocacy encompasses the realm of seeds and their regenerative capacity, and also the preservation of traditional cultures and lands. These two threads, when woven together, are fundamental to creating a more viable sustainable food system through the preservation of diversity—both biological and cultural. "The work of seed savers, traditional farmers, medicinal plant healers, and the new food movement is so inspiring. But it is what women have been doing all along—sustaining life on earth," says Claire.

Working with indigenous peoples across Asia, North America, and Hawaii, Claire has played an integral part in the environmental, food, and farming movement for over thirty years. Her weekly Bay Area Food and Farming show on KPFA-FM began in 1998 before the term "local" was even in season, educating hundreds of thousands of listeners about the importance of sustainable food and agriculture. Her career in journalism began in Vietnam, and today she continues inspiring people to advocate for change through her writing and broadcasting. For fifteen years she has been reporting on the technologies that help us and those that could harm us, as well as telling the stories that help us understand the importance of putting the "culture" back into "agriculture." Her award-wining book, *Uncertain Peril,* is a testament to her dedication in advocating for the integrity of the natural world and the cultures that honor the essential relationship between people, plants, and place.

Claire's activism began in 1964 when she was a student at UC Berkeley, a time when social turmoil, especially the peace movement, was very much a part of public life. She heard Cesar Chavez, Martin Luther King Jr., and feminists speak out against human rights injustices. They helped form a new perspective and outlook for Claire. "My being a social activist in Berkeley in the 1960s gave me a broader point of view, showing me that we are connected to something larger than our own lives and that there are diverse world views behind these issues. And peoples' lives are at stake. As a result, I believe we have a moral imperative to help others and not just live for ourselves."

> "I believe we have a moral imperative to help others and not just live for ourselves."

Later in the 1960s Claire was drawn into the "back to the land" movement. She wanted to be a farmer. "I had always felt the calling to do something on the land. But women of my generation were not empowered to act on their own dreams. We thought that if you didn't think you could do it yourself, you should marry someone who could," she says, laughing. So she married a farmer.

The couple lived on a farm outside Davis in 1968, then moved to the Sacramento Valley to farm rice, and in the early 1970s moved to the Napa Valley to grow grapes. During that time Claire raised three children all while keeping a place in her heart for activism. She marched in antiwar rallies with her children, one in a backpack and another in a stroller. In the rural communities where she lived, she worked for farm worker rights, inspired by the teachings of Chavez and King.

FIGHTING FOR NATIVE LAND RIGHTS

When her marriage ended, Claire moved back to the San Francisco Bay Area to attend law school and focus on her social justice work. After Claire graduated from law school, she held an honors appointment with the Carter administration as staff counsel for the United States Department of Agriculture (USDA). Several important influences came together at that time and determined how she worked as a lawyer. Her love of nature, the influence of her father (who had worked and lived with American Indians in the early twentieth century), her studies in cultural anthropology at Berkeley and Davis, and her activism all melded to form her future career as an indigenous land rights advocate. While at the USDA she practiced environmental law and was given work where she was able to save sacred sites on National Forest land for both the cultures of the past and living native peoples. In 1980 she read an important court decision about Navajo and Hopi cultural sites on a mountain in Arizona (the Snow Bowl decision). At the time, others in her office were working on the other side of the issue—supporting development on native lands in Northern California (the G-O Road decision). Claire recognized the need for legal advocacy to preserve sacred sites and decided to leave government practice in order to represent traditional native people in court and to advocate for them in the emergent land trust movement. In addition to founding The Cultural Conservancy, a Native land rights organization (see Melissa Nelson, page 156), she litigated and advised tribes and traditional groups about how to use historic preservation laws to protect their cultural values.

Working with these communities was a profound experience. She was invited to participate in various ceremonies and became connected to the people she met through their stories, traditions, and rituals, which communicated their abiding respect for natural cycles. Claire had found a place as an advocate that combined her passion for cultural diversity and the integrity of the land. "At the time," she says, "Reagan was waging his anti-environment and deregulation campaigns—changes that are at the heart of many of our social and environmental problems today."

Claire used her legal skills to protect Native cultural practices and land rights on both public and private land. "American law is all about protecting private property," says Claire, "and it does not recognize the immanent or transcendent, complex spiritual values—a sacred geography, as it were, that is integral to land-based traditional cultures." Her work recognized both the environmental and spiritual traditions of people, an effort that has ultimately created more legal recourse for tribes. "I was the first to draft a cultural conservation easement to protect sacred sites on private land and to form native land trusts. In court, I represented both environmental and indigenous groups in cases that were brought to protect places—their biological diversity and cultural diversity. It was an amazing experience," she says.

"The real work was always about figuring out innovative ways to fit a completely different worldview into the western legal framework," says Claire. "For instance, I would not use anthropologists as the 'experts.' I worked to qualify the traditional elders in that position so the court could get valuable cultural information directly, and I used the academic experts as translators for the elders. Just gathering the evidence would take months of research, and my training in cultural anthropology was helpful."

Some of Claire's projects included working with the traditional San Carlos Apache fighting telescopes on Mount Graham in Arizona, representing them against the U.S. Forest Service; trying to stop a major freeway project on the island of Oahu that would have destroyed the last intact native plants and cultural sites of Halawa Valley; and starting the first Native land trust in Hana, Maui. She also worked to protect the Green Corn Ceremony for the traditional Seminole in Florida; to save a sacred water site near Taos, New Mexico, for the Taos Pueblo; and to stop mining in the Sweetgrass Hills for the Blackfoot people. Perhaps her best known work was on behalf of the Winnemem Wintu in northern California, where she successfully stopped development of a ski resort on their sacred Panther Meadows on Mount Shasta.

Despite the challenging nature of this work, each of these experiences built incredibly powerful friendships and relationships with native people that sustained and invigorated her. These heart-based components of her work fueled her commitment to defending the sacred earth. "For me, it has been an enormous privilege to be a witness to these fast disappearing lifeways and traditional people, especially Florence Jones, a nationally recognized Wintu healer who came from a long line of women herbal doctors in northern California. And ultimately, for me, it's always been about the relationship between people and the land," says Claire. Today, over twenty-five years later, these experiences and relationships with traditional practitioners are still what she values most.

FIGHTING BIOTECHNOLOGY

Claire made remarkable progress as an advocate for indigenous rights within the confines of the legal system. However, the role of government and the legacy of President Reagan continued their harmful impacts on the integrity of nature and our very culture. Reagan changed the role of government from protecting human rights and reining in greedy business interests to being the cohort of some of the worst corporate crimes ever. One story in particular caught Claire's attention: the way the biotechnology industry took over food and farming.

The same year as Reagan's inauguration, 1980, a little-known but important law was passed, The Bayh-Dole Act. For the first time in our history, patents were allowed on the results of research done with public money at public universities. This law increased special interest research and allowed corporations and the universities to keep the patents, and profits, even though the intellectual infrastructure and talent for this innovation was supplied by the public and paid for by taxpayers. Claire studied the changes made by the Reagan and Bush administrations as they became part of a right wing backlash against the social and human rights progress made in the 1960s and '70s. The Bayh-Dole Act is just one example, but it's a major reason why biotechnology has come to dominate food and farming, as it allowed corporations to take over our research institutions. It opened a Pandora's box of gene manipulation and the patenting of life, even while using the very public institutions that should be protecting public health and interests.

As Claire articulates in her book, *Uncertain Peril,* biotechnology is a form of violence against the natural world. It is colonialism, she explains. It is the exact same thing that happened over the last five hundred years, as trading companies, military, and colonial powers barged into indigenous lands and took the land, the water, the trees— purposefully destroying land-based cultures. Biotechnology is bio-colonialism. It takes any form of natural life and presumes to mix and match species and manufacture artificially modified and patented products that are owned and commercialized for profit. Companies claim the biotechnology can do some good, such as feeding people or curing disease. But the fact is that after thirty years and billions of dollars of research, nothing has come of this technology except products that harm the environment and human health.

Now so many of the beautiful and useful gifts of nature—plants, mammals, insects, birds, fish—have been modified and patented, meaning that they are privately owned and controlled. Staple crops like corn, wheat, and rice have all been genetically modified and patented, and the genomes are now owned by private companies. Our traditionally bred plants and publicly funded seed research has been upstaged by large biotech agrochemical companies such as Monsanto, DuPont/Pioneer Hi-Bred, Syngenta, and Dow.[1]

This is a chilling scenario, because whoever controls the future of seeds, says Claire, controls the future of food and perhaps even the means to support all life on earth. This has led Claire to expose yet another layer of injustice and to advocate for an even deeper need for respect for the inherent integrity of the natural world. She says that "seeds contain both biological and cultural information, and the way we treat seeds is a reflection of how we treat ourselves. Ultimately, if we cannot find a way to sustain cultural diversity, our biological diversity will fail as well."

"Seeds," says Claire in her book, "are messengers from the past. They endure because they are generous. They survive by being resilient, abundant, and adaptable. The story of seeds is also our story. . . . What we do to seeds, we do to ourselves."[2]

STORYTELLER FOR SUSTAINABILITY

Claire's work over the past forty-plus years has been challenging and invigorating. Her interactions with people and cultures around the world and the inspiration that she continues to share through her presentations, speaking engagements, and publications helps shine a light on the truths behind our current agricultural system, both local and global. "A lot of my work is telling the stories that make the links between things. It's all about making connections for people, making sure they have both the facts and context. It's just not good enough to grow food organically so a few of us can eat better. As many writers are now pointing out in their critiques of 'industrial organic' (large scale, non-diversified, organic farms), farmers need to understand the connections between the land, the biodiversity, and the cultural relationships that are part of the natural world."

"Farmers need to understand the connections between the land, the biodiversity, and the cultural relationships that are part of the natural world."

As a journalist, Claire continues to work at the forefront of the stories she covers. She remembers vividly the experience of going into one of the pressrooms of a biotechnology industry convention and seeing the incredible array of press information clearly articulating their arguments for the establishment of GMOs (genetically modified organisms). When she left, she told her colleagues in the anti-biotechnology and pro-sustainable agriculture community, "We need to establish our own relationships with the press." So she wrote the first press guide to agricultural biotechnology that provided mainstream press with experts and scientists who could critique the technology. "We have our own experts and we all need to be better storytellers," she says. She then went on to write *Uncertain Peril*, now widely praised for its insights into the origins of biotechnology, the stories of its impacts on farmers and rural communities, and the land and cultures that are irrevocably damaged. She has gone on to galvanize support for a return to preserving our natural systems and respecting both the genius of nature as well as human ingenuity.

Claire's vision for the future is to "see a return of respect for traditional farming and indigenous knowledge, in cooperation with the newer forms of sustainable agriculture and new sustainable technologies such as biomimicry and organic farming. As human societies, we can reconnect and reestablish the precious interrelationships between people, plants, and place that have always sustained us.

"In so many ways," continues Claire, "industrial agriculture has been the source of social problems, pollution, poor health, poverty, and the domination of nature. When we realize how fundamental food and farming are to human life, we can begin to see that the way we eat is not just the problem, but also the solution. By changing just this one aspect of our lives—how we feed ourselves—we can restore our personal and planetary health, the integrity of the natural world, and our right relation to it."

> "The way we eat is not just the problem, but also the solution."

Suzanne Ashworth
Seed Saver, Del Rio Botanical

In an effort to protect our seeds from corporations and to ensure seed diversity, it's necessary to engage farmers in the preservation of seed varieties. As it is now, patents on seed varieties have made innumerous genomes that have been part of cultures the world over for thousands of years the property of corporations. While not every farmer has her own seed library, Suzanne Ashworth does. She is an example of a farmer that not only saves seeds and grows unique heirloom varieties of foods, but who also extends her knowledge to others as well.

Growing up on her farm just below the levee on the Sacramento River, Suzanne is a third-generation family farmer dedicated to educating and preserving seed diversity. Her book, Seed to Seed: Seed Saving and Growing Techniques for Vegetable Gardeners, tells all of us exactly what seed companies don't want us to know: how to save seed. A "seed curator" for the organization Seed Savers Exchange, she gifted the rights of the book to the organization. Seed Savers Exchange members have interchanged an estimated one million seed samples from gardener to gardener since 1975. This has made Suzanne's book an indispensable resource compiled from her numerous years of conducting seed trials and collecting information from obscure texts of seed saving logistics. She shares her passion for diversity and plants with the rest of us with her vibrant seed library of beans, mustards, squashes, tomatoes, and every other imaginable legume, brassica, composite, cucurbita, and solanum.

ANNA LAPPÉ

AUTHOR, *DIET FOR A HOT PLANET*

ADVOCATE, SMALL PLANET INSTITUTE

The Small Planet Institute is an organization that promotes the creation of "living democracies" in which people actively work toward creating the kinds of societal rules and norms that reflect their values.

While growing up in the Bay Area, the question of what to eat was answered by Anna's mom, Frances Moore Lappé, author of *Diet for a Small Planet*. Frances was committed to feeding her family whole grains, plenty of fresh fruits and vegetables, and mostly vegetarian made-from-scratch foods that were largely organic—which she did on top of working full time and being a single mother. Table talk during dinner frequently included conversations of social and environmental justice, served with a side dish of the detrimental impacts the agriculture and chemical industries have on the environment and human health. These conversations and upbringing would ultimately influence and set in motion her work of advocacy as an adult.

HOPE'S EDGE

After finishing her master's degree, Anna joined forces with her mom in 2000 to write the sequel to *Diet for a Small Planet,* called *Hope's Edge: The Next Diet for a Small Planet*. Research for the book led Anna and Frances on a yearlong whirlwind tour of urban and rural farms throughout the United States, India, Brazil, Kenya, France, and Poland. Every day they met with farmers, community members, and agricultural professionals to get the scoop on the global sustainable food movement. What Anna and Frances found through their travels were the inspiring stories of food relocalization, of people bringing their food closer to home through urban farming, farmer collectives, and the preservation of traditional seed varieties and farming techniques. Whether government- or community-supported, these activities are giving people a greater sense of food security and preserving their countries' cultural food traditions.

"It was that particular experience that set me on this path," remembers Anna, finding the truth in her mother's message that the root of hunger is not a scarcity of food, but a scarcity of democracy. Their efforts couldn't have been more appropriately timed. The global food crisis hit the headlines in June of 2009, proclaiming that nearly one-sixth of the world's population, some 1.02 billion people, were going hungry.[3]

COOKING FOR SOLUTIONS

While Anna fondly remembers the food her mother made for her and her brother from scratch, she wouldn't gain her full-fledged culinary gusto until living in France in 2002. Getting schooled by Eric (her French boyfriend) in the open-air markets of Paris on the ripeness of melons, the way to caress an avocado to determine its readiness, and how to avoid fruits and veggies past their prime, Anna's confidence and culinary repertoire in the kitchen grew. Falling in love with the Parisian gestalt for food, she settled into an apartment for nine months to focus on writing *Hope's Edge*. She lived next door to a six-day-a-week open-air market, and while the vendors weren't necessarily local or organic, it was such a new experience living in a city where people shopped for their food on a daily basis. "You would decide what you wanted for dinner that night and go shopping, and then stop by the wine shop and tell the woman what you were making, and she would recommend the most amazing bottle of $4 wine," says Anna.

Eric's family welcomed her warmly into their circle, inviting her to their endless Sunday dinners, leisurely experiences that started in the afternoon and wrapped up late in the evening. What's more was that the prices of foods that are considered gourmet or elite in the U.S. were affordable so that the majority of people, no matter what their income, could access really delicious foods (especially cheese). "We would get basic foods at this market, and there were over 150 varieties of cheeses," she remembers. Anna contrasts the difference of American markets of a similar economic bracket as stark in comparison: the U.S. has quite a way to go before the average Safeway, Kroger, or Dominick's serves up such an *affordable* selection of handmade products.

Back at home, she noticed that highly processed foods and refined flour and corn syrup dominated the shelves, a fact that presented itself repeatedly while Anna was researching for her book *Grub,* which she co-authored with Bryant Terry.

Anna observed while in France that even one of the most gastronomic countries in the world is not immune to Western food culture. McDonald's, Quick Burger, and other fast food companies are making an inroad through the current generations. She explains that as France's economy changes, there is added pressure to extend the country's thirty-five hour work week, and that the two-hour lunch is starting to take a back seat to capitalism.

FOOD OR FUEL?

These days, you can't really talk about food without mentioning those compacted dinosaur parts that make up our oil supply. Oil allows us to ship food, and byproducts of refining oil become fertilizers, pesticides, and herbicides. The Food and Agriculture Organization (FAO) of the United Nations publishes a Global Food Price Index, which clearly illustrates the impact that oil prices have on the cost of various foods. The oil spike in April and June of 2008 exemplifies this point well. When the FAO revisited the index in October 2008, they found that although oil prices had dropped from those in early April, food prices were still 28 percent higher than in October 2006.[4] Fuel inevitably determines the affordability of food due to shipping, harvesting, water pumping and other on-farm diesel needs as well as those chemical inputs that all affect food prices. The FAO also found a decline in food assistance to developing countries during peak oil times, assumed to be due to shipping costs and restrictions on domestic supply as grain stocks dwindle. Developing countries with food insecurity need to look at local food-growing alternatives now to address global food shortages.

"What drew me to climate change was discovering the research from the FAO that livestock production alone accounts for 18 percent of global warming, more than all global transportation. The food system as a whole is responsible for as much as one-third of global emissions," says Anna. "Once you see the downside of the food system and emissions impact, the next question is whether there's a way to reduce this. We know what is needed to reduce emissions from the food sector; we have the know-how to grow sustainable food," she says.

Biofuels from plant matter that are being heavily endorsed by politicians and corporations alike present another obstacle in our capacity to feed the growing population as arable land, water, and other precious natural resources are used to grow crops for fuel versus food. This phenomenon is happening most frequently in the United States but also in other agricultural economies such as Brazil and Argentina. Anna points out that this system is not energy efficient and doesn't make the best use of land. By her estimates, it takes as much as one and a half tons of natural gas to produce one ton of synthetic nitrogen that is needed to grow corn for biofuels. After these fertilizers, processing, and shipping are taken into account, the math of energy inputs versus outputs just doesn't add up.

A report from Food and Water Watch found that "the most favorable estimates, which already include cellulosic feedstocks (i.e. corn), point out that fuel made from biomass can replace only one-fourth to one-third of transport-related oil consumption."[5] The Institute for Agriculture and Trade Policy backs these claims and points out that genetically modified corn, rejected on the global market, is now going into ethanol as well. In a time of food shortages, squandering our land, water, and climate for corn destined for fuel, not food, is a real crime—and one that, incidentally, wouldn't be possible without the U.S. Farm Bill subsidizing the crop.

"We need to help create a global food system," says Anna, "one that provides food for all, creates a healthy climate, and promotes biodiversity." The answer is already in action as roughly two billion people still engage in subsistence farming the world over to feed themselves and their families.[6] We can support these small-scale farmers by providing them with information, education, and basic technologies and celebrating them for their important work as stewards

"Scarcity of food is a scarcity of democracy."

of the land. They are part of the key solution to climate change and are providers of food security to rural and urban populations alike.

During Anna's travels and research, she's made a point to hear the "other side of the coin," the agribusiness spin on food, fuel, and the future. She has read Syngenta's sustainability plans, has watched Monsanto's advertising videos about how they plan to "feed the world," and has attended many agribusiness conferences.

"If anything," she says, "it's proven to me that we [the sustainable agriculture movement] really are right and that we do have the answers." Yet she still reminds everyone to not get fixated on their own perspectives and blind themselves to these ongoing discussions. The corporations certainly aren't going to disappear tomorrow, especially with the proliferation of the mindset that their technologies are what the world needs to feed itself. Their monetary investments are sadly speaking louder than the science that is proving organic and sustainable agriculture can really feed the world.

IT'S A SMALL PLANET

Anna has extended herself beyond the reaches of her devoted readership to help fund the movement for a vibrant and resilient food system. She started the Small Planet Fund in 2002 with her mother, to support grassroots organizations working towards greater food security for people who lack sufficient food and land resources. Harnessing contributions from hundreds of small-scale donors, the two have helped raise more than $500,000 dollars since the organization's inception.

Anna's work and international experience have led her to the point she is at today as a spokesperson for food system change and a whistleblower on the inefficiencies of "modern" agriculture. Her latest book, *Diet for a Hot Planet: The Climate Crisis at the End of Our Fork and What We Can Do About It* (Bloomsbury 2010), addresses food from the perspective of climate change.

DEBORAH KOONS GARCIA

FOUNDER, LILY FILMS

DIRECTOR, *THE FUTURE OF FOOD* AND *SYMPHONY OF THE SOIL*

The Future of Food is a documentary that exposes the startling problems of our industrial food system. *Symphony of the Soil* explores humans' relationship with soil.

"It's up to you" is the last line shown on the screen of Deborah Koons Garcia's debut documentary, *The Future of Food*. Providing critical insight into the potential problems with genetically modified crops and food (GMOs), food that has silently filled the shelves of grocery stores and pantries across the United States, the film documents the unhealthy evolution of our agricultural system: planes fly over fields dusting crops with pesticides and herbicides; children run through DDT in New York; farmers get sued by corporations; and the "revolving door" of corporate professionals-turned-government-appointees are exposed. Upon the film's release in 2004, it received accolades, played at many food and farming film festivals, and was designated one of the best documentaries of the year by the Academy Awards screening committee. Heralded as the *Silent Spring* of food, *The Future of Food* and its filmmaker, Deborah Koons Garcia, have shown that the power of media can educate and create change both in people's personal lives and in policy.

Deborah fell in love with filmmaking in 1970 while a student at the University of North Carolina, Chapel Hill, where she became a conscientious eater and vegetarian. "I was studying English, and as soon as I picked up a 16 mm Bolex camera, that was it," she says. In the mid-1970s, she moved to San Francisco, earned a Master of Fine Arts from the San Francisco Art Institute, and continued making both fiction and documentary films.

She had always wanted to make a film about the differences between organic and chemical agriculture and began researching about the changes that occur in endocrine systems because of pesticide use.

As she dug into the issue, she started to learn about corporations like Monsanto that were genetically engineering crops, buying up seed companies, patenting life, and suing farmers. "The focus of the film shifted," she remembers. "I was shocked to find out what was happening and shocked that I did not know about it since I was very informed about food matters. In the United States, this was happening totally under the radar. Just like the corporations wanted it to be. I was determined to change that."

"You have to engage people emotionally and get underneath the surface stuff."

The Future of Food made its way throughout America and spread like wildfire around the globe and has been seen by millions of people. The distribution has been unique and groundbreaking: the Japanese version was translated by Japan Organics, the farming organization; the Soil Association of the United Kingdom sponsored the premier in London; and one farmer with a CSA in the United States bought four thousand copies to give to all of his members.

To help get the information in the film out to the public, Deborah has given hundreds of interviews. She became an informal advisor to concerned citizens who had never organized a public event and helped them plan movie showings, panels, and related activities. "I told them I would show up but they would have to do everything else. They all loved the experience—they made new friends and really felt part of their communities." Many of the organizers planned food receptions that featured local farmers and restaurants. One of Deborah's favorite showings happened in Spokane, Washington, where a local chef prepared dinner for two hundred filmgoers/community members using only ingredients from within a fifty-mile radius—for free! This brought farmers, producers, and the community together to celebrate their local options for countering corporate control of our food. After the Davis, California, showing (co-sponsored by CAFF, Slow Food, and Organic Sacramento), a protest was organized in front of the Monsanto building located downtown. Davis, a world-renowned agricultural research university, was mentioned in the movie since many large seed companies are located nearby. These companies fund and develop seed stocks using the university's facilities, staff, and students—just one of the realities exposed in the film.

The Future of Food created community organizers overnight; people enraged about the U.S. government's pro-GMO stance created solutions they could enact. "I've met several people who have started farmers markets after seeing the movie, saying, 'We need one of those in our town.' Other people write and say, 'I joined a CSA, I cleared out my cupboard of processed foods.' There are so many ways for people to get involved," says Deborah.

One of the most remarkable aspects of the film is the credit it gets for helping to pass Measure H, a ban on the growing of GMO crops or animals, in Mendocino County, California. In March of 2004, Mendocino became the first county to ban the growing of GMOs, even though the proponents were grossly outspent by the biotech industry.

Today, just four behemoth agrochemical and seed corporations—Syngenta, Dow, Monsanto, and DuPont/Pioneer Hi-Bred—own 85 percent of the world's seed supply.[7] They have purchased almost all of the world's seed-producing facilities and have been busy submitting patents for native varieties of plants and animals around the world. The public, and especially Native tribes of the U.S. and beyond, are resisting this patenting by creating seed libraries, cataloging their diversity, and by standing up to these huge multinational corporations.

The first patent that opened the floodgates to patenting DNA was on a genetically engineered oil-eating bacteria.[8] The Supreme Court affirmed the right of the scientist to patent this "discovery" and thus ultimately allowed the patenting of all forms of life—whether they had been existing for thousands of years or not. Companies are now able to lock up the rights to the DNA, the genetic code of thousands of varieties of seeds. This means that if they decided to reduce their "stock," which they often do out of monetary reasons, we lose access to these varieties forever—a chilling scenario. Seeds should be a public good and should be maintained by

Companies are now able to lock up the rights to the DNA, the genetic code of thousands of varieties of seeds.

a public entity such as our land grant institutions that receive federal money, not private corporations.

The four major crops that are genetically engineered today are corn, soybeans, cotton, and canola. Since corn is a large staple for feedlot animals, the material is also found in non-organic meat products. Another sneaky place where GMOs are found is in more than 80 percent of processed foods via corn and soy byproducts, most commonly as corn syrup and soy lecithin.[9] Since labeling of GMOs is not mandatory in the States (Europe passed mandatory labeling years ago), the best way to avoid eating processed foods is by purchasing organic foods. Efforts by consumer watchdog groups such as the Organic Consumers Association to implement mandatory labeling in the United States have been repeatedly blocked by GMO lobbyists.

THE MEDIA AS A TOOL FOR OUTREACH

Deborah believes that media—both good filmmaking and the web—are keys to providing us with the truth that we deserve. "Whether it's a movie or rock show, media and outreach are keys to success," says Deborah. This is something she learned early on in her marriage to Grateful Dead guitarist Jerry Garcia. She was amazed at how much time he spent giving interviews and realized how important this was to his great success as a musician. "Jerry told me he talked to journalists as if they were people," says Deborah jokingly. During her outreach for the film, Deborah was surprised at how genuinely interested journalists were in the subject and found a much greater attention to detail and accuracy in reporting on her film and the issues at hand than the fantastical approach she had witnessed in the entertainment arena. "In the world of rock and roll you find people making stuff up all the time, and for some reason, when dealing with the food and farming world, people really want to get it right. They care about their food and want to understand the food system. It makes me think that I did something right when I saw this attitude of openness. That's why I did the film, to be a conduit for the issues."

Today there are so many ways to get information beyond just film and TV. This is the time when online campaigns can win elections, ban battery cages for hens (California's Proposition 2), educate people about industrialized farms, and keep everyone up to date (in varying degrees of journalism) through blogs, social networking sites, and emails. However, with all that information "stuff" out there, there's a lot to filter through and an even greater need to bring people together face to face to discuss issues and determine action. Deborah did just that through *The Future of Food* and plans to do it again with her next feature about the beauty and celebration of our natural system's resiliency. *Symphony of the Soil,* Deborah's latest film, explores the connection we have with one of nature's most mysterious living organisms.

> "Appreciating the natural beauty right now will open our hearts and fortify us for all we must do."

While *The Future of Food* helped put the brakes on Monsanto, Cargill, and Syngenta's biotechnology agenda, *Symphony of the Soil* explores the potential we have to make it right again with one of Earth's most fundamental resources—soil.

The film substantiates the importance of soil's role in our ecosystem as one of our most paramount resources in the solutions to a multitude of global environmental issues, including climate change, erosion, and food production capacity. "We are all part of the soil community, and if we treated soil right we could we could turn this poor degraded planet into a garden," says Deborah.

Deborah continues to educate with compassion for the people and the land that bring all of us so much abundance, saying, "I can look out on my orchard and the fruit trees start blossoming, spring comes and there's a relentless quality that things will be reborn. Those are the pear flowers, those will be pears. Appreciating the natural beauty right now will open our hearts and fortify us for all we must do. That's what we need right now."

GLENDA
HUMISTON

CALIFORNIA'S
STATE DIRECTOR
OF USDA'S RURAL
DEVELOPMENT
PROGRAMS

FORMER DEPUTY
UNDER SECRETARY
FOR NATURAL
RESOURCES AND
ENVIRONMENT
AT THE U.S.
DEPARTMENT OF
AGRICULTURE

Glenda advocates for
farmland preservation,
water quality enhance-
ment, and improved natu-
ral resources management

Mark Twain's infamous quote, "Whiskey is for drinking, water is for fighting over," pretty much sums up Glenda Humiston's upbringing on her family ranch in Colorado and policy work as an adult. Not the drinking part, but the sticky business of negotiating water, land, and ownership between citizens, government agencies, and nonprofit organizations that often spend more time litigating their issues than talking about them around a table.

Perhaps one of her biggest accomplishments in working towards a more sustainable food system has been to reverse this litigation trend by facilitating conversations with diverse shareholders. By doing so, and by writing recommendations in language that people can understand, she has worked tenaciously to close the gap between the government and public. In between earning a master's degree in International Agricultural Development and completing her recent Ph.D. program, Glenda has logged nearly twenty years working at local, state, and federal levels for farmland preservation, water quality enhancement, and improved natural resources management as a nonprofit executive, consultant, and Deputy Under Secretary for Natural Resources and Environment at the U.S. Department of Agriculture in Washington D.C.

As the eldest of five girls, Glenda took responsibility as a youth for keeping the family ranch running while her father served as a water commissioner for southwest Colorado. Glenda's parents farmed the original homestead ranch of two hundred acres, while her grandfather's ranch provided 160 acres more suitable for growing hay and other feed crops. The Humiston family also utilized an additional five hundred acres in forest service territory to raise their free ranging grassfed beef.

Growing up on the land and in water and cattle country, Glenda credits her success in working with diverse coalitions to growing up with 4-H and FFA (Future Farmers of America), where she learned fundamental facilitation tools in their "parliamentary procedure" lessons. Through this experience and with encouragement from her father to get into politics, Glenda learned that a leader's job is to get everyone in the room on the same page, but also to make sure that all voices are heard fairly. These are skills that, according to Glenda, most people don't get a chance to cultivate.

CREATING POLICY WITH THE PEOPLE

How would you get environmentalists, landowners, and policy makers to work together to create a land use plan in California? The answer for the state of California in the '90s was to bring in Glenda, a consultant at the time with AGvocate Consulting Services. According to Glenda, up until that point, land use policies and plans were usually created by "agency staffers that would go into their cubicles and write up a plan for water or land use, would get technical data from an aide or two, and then throw it out to the public for review—giving them thirty to forty-five days at most. The public is usually blindsided and angry. Who can read through three hundred pages of bureaucratic language in that timeframe anyway? Someone would file a lawsuit and the fight would be on," she says.

Policy created without transparency and public buy-in, according to Glenda, almost always ends up in court, a truth that she can't stand. "They accomplish nothing and by the time the 'battle' is over, the resource that everyone was worried about protecting has been lost and the funds have dried up," she says.

One of her first consulting projects—for the state's Range Management Advisory Committee—would turn the aforementioned process on its head. It gave Glenda the chance to create a plan that would improve land stewardship and meet water quality compliance goals of the 1990 Coastal Zone Act Reauthorization Amendment

(CZARA) by the grazing and ranching community. Although the federal Clean Water Act and California's Porter-Cologne Act were the guiding forces regulating water quality at that time, CZARA took on a powerful role when the State of California chose to classify the entire state as a "coastal zone." Although this action initially alarmed many farming interests, Glenda quickly realized that it was a huge opportunity for the agricultural community to get ahead of the regulatory curve for a change. As she points out, "CZARA was based on the notion that farmers and ranchers that implemented 'Best Management Practices' (BMPs) would be doing the right thing for the environment and would—in essence—be innocent until proven guilty. This was the opposite from how the Clean Water Act programs were being administered."

For Glenda, the challenge would be getting various state and federal agencies, diverse interest groups, and others in the public and private sectors together for consensus building. She decided to get buy-in from the various stakeholders from the start and then "take the proposal on the road to communities throughout the state" to get further buy-in from the public. Her first action was to create a policy and technical advisory committee to review existing policies and programs and the type of BMPs that were available to landowners. She also explored recommendations on how to help landowners improve their water and land management conservation practices.

The Advisory Committee, comprising roughly seventy people, performed well during their first meeting when they examined all of the existing types of Best Management Practices (BMPs) that a landowner might use to meet the goals of CZARA. At the second meeting, Glenda took that list of BMPs and juxtaposed a list of all of the permits that a farmer or landowner might need to obtain in order to actually implement them. The permit requirements were so confusing and noncorresponding with each other that even the agency representatives who had jurisdiction over the permit programs weren't sure of the landowner requirements. And if they couldn't understand, how was anyone else supposed to? And, although the Rangeland Water Quality Plan was aimed mostly at cattle and sheep ranchers, many of these same barriers were actually affecting conservation groups' efforts to implement environmental projects as well.

After the third meeting—at which the group brainstormed some tentative solutions and discussed the need for ongoing monitoring— Glenda traveled to various parts of California, pulling together agencies and others concerned with conservation on private property to get their feedback. In addition to presenting the Advisory Committee's tentative ideas and gathering feedback, she collected a number of best practices she discovered while traveling throughout the state.

For example, in Sonoma County, the Farm Bureau was administering a "peer pressure" program with local farmers volunteering to meet with other farmers that might not be meeting current regulations. Agencies, such as the Department of Fish and Game, would report a potential problem to the Farm Bureau and allow the peers to attempt a resolution before initiating regulatory citations. The farmers that volunteered had personal relationships in their community of non-complying farmers and ranchers. This way, they could share their own experience with use of BMPs and other conservation tools. This peer pressure was free and quick and resulted in far more frequent implementation of good conservation practices than confrontations. It also opened the dialogue for more communication between people in the community—a much different approach than a regulatory agency just showing up on your farm.

Another example of what she gleaned was the involvement of high school classes that used class hours to monitor watersheds and compile data from water quality surveys. This provided students with hands-on activities that met state curriculum standards for science coursework, and inexpensive monitoring for the state—a win-win program.

After she finished this tour in 1994, Glenda returned home to begin writing the California Rangeland Water Quality Management Plan, which would ultimately include not only the plan itself but extensive appendices that explained the various BMPs, including how to decide which actions to take; how to fund and implement the practices; and how to monitor results. Examples of actual plans ranged from very simple to complex and allowed the ranchers and other landowners to easily determine how they could comply with the requirements of CZARA. Glenda broke it down for everyone "in plain English. These are the practices, these are the regulations, here's how we need to change things." This was a huge change from the plans' bureaucratic jargon of yesteryear that required a law degree to understand. The reaction to the final document was universally positive with regulatory agencies, environmental groups, and the ranching communities, who appreciated the way she was able to increase the transparency of the process and achieve ownership of the plan by all the stakeholders she met with.

The State Water Resources Control Board applauded her work and her ability to create such consensus on a subject that had been fraught with controversy. During the actual presentation of the plan, groups that usually sat on different sides of the environmental/landowner fence such as the Pacific Institute, the California Cattlemen's Association, and the EPA all explained why this Rangeland Water Quality Management Plan would meet the goals established by the CZARA and even exceed them. Each recognized how the plan would be a great resource in the improvement of land management practices and protection of the state's precious water resources. They noted that many ranchers were already actively implementing the plan's recommendations.

After wrapping up the plan, Glenda continued her work as a consultant for other agencies and organizations. She involved herself deeper in public service in such roles as commissioner on the Sonoma County Local Agency Formation Commission (LAFCo) and president of the California Association of Resource Conservations Districts (CARCD). (Resource Conservation Districts are local independent special districts authorized by the state to facilitate delivery of USDA conservation programs and lead local efforts to conserve our natural resources.)

Glenda had been steadily climbing in the leadership ranks of CARCD all the way to vice president until it was time for her to serve as president. She put together a statewide campaign for her seat when some of the conservative elements within the organization decided they would back another candidate. "They didn't mind me being vice president," said Glenda, "but when it was time to step up to become president, well, I was young (thirty-seven), a woman, a Democrat, and an out lesbian. A few folks weren't really excited about all that, although it's really hard to know which characteristic was the most problematic!" Despite the overall conservative nature of the Districts, Glenda managed to win the election with over 70 percent of the vote, and she successfully led CARCD for the next eighteen months.

Then, in 1998, Glenda headed to the other coast when offered an appointment from President Clinton to serve as Deputy Under Secretary for Natural Resources and Environment at the U.S. Department of Agriculture in Washington, D.C. Glenda suddenly found herself working eighty-hour weeks for our nation's politicos. She loved everything about it—the pace, the wide array of projects, the opportunity to oversee an agency with a $1.4 billion dollar budget and more than eleven thousand employees. "I was able to handle it because I had so much community organizing experience, a strong technological background, and intimate knowledge of these particular policies and programs. Plus, I had already established a broad network of supportive colleagues. I have to admit, sometimes I felt in over my head in Washington, but I found that I was quite good at juggling all the various interests and issues," says Glenda. The experience provided unparalleled opportunities to expand her knowledge and understanding of the many complex issues that inhabit federal food and agricultural policy, and it fueled her desire to explore new ideas that could help lead to a greater proliferation of sustainable agriculture in the U.S.

FARM BILL REFORM

It seemed clear to Glenda that the U.S. Farm Bill was ripe for reform, particularly after the 2002 Farm Bill had angered so many interest groups and appeared to be violating agreements made within the World Trade Organization. During the debates leading up to the 2008 Farm Bill, the process was notable for the engagement of many new and quite diverse interest groups as well as unprecedented media coverage of farm policy issues. This led her to focus her Ph.D. at UC Berkeley on analyzing the motivations and actions of key interest groups, the means used to influence policy, and how various interests reacted to policy initiatives within the 2008 Farm Bill.

Glenda's findings point out that, rather than engaging in comprehensive policy reforms, Congress was constantly responding to the demands of powerful competing interests. She believes there are several lessons to be learned from recent reform campaigns that can be effectively exploited in the effort to enact reform in the 2012 Farm Bill. "The 'reform coalitions' approach in the 2008 Farm Bill was all too often direct confrontation with the Farm Bloc's vested interests [such as the Cotton Council and Farm Bureau], the USDA agencies, and the House and Senate Agriculture Committees," she explained. "In essence, the reform coalition tried to pressure the legislature while bypassing the agencies and the vested interest groups. They largely failed."

Between now and the next Farm Bill, Glenda acknowledges that there are "a lot of challenges happening for our farmers: environmental impacts of climate change, drought, invasive species, deflated prices on the global market, and the possibility of going bankrupt. You can't keep farming if you lose money every year." Glenda's own family farm now runs fewer than one hundred cow-calf pairs on the ranch—not enough to support a family these days. The family has recently begun to host a large motorcycle rally on the ranch over Labor Day weekend to create income and—they hope—allow them to keep the ranch in the family. Glenda's dad still talks about water issues over dinner, but now the issues are complicated by rapid population growth in the area and an enduring drought.

"You can't keep farming if you lose money every year."

With all these changes and challenges, it's good to know that there are people with land-based experience like Glenda serving in leadership positions. Such experience is increasingly rare, and it brings a whole new dimension to her work of facilitating the sustainable food movement. Now that the Ph.D. is done, Glenda looks forward to working on various efforts to create sustainability in our agriculture as

well as our communities. As she puts it, "Despite what reform may—
or may not—have been incorporated into the 2008 Farm Bill, more
important in the long run is the entry of so many new interest groups
and the heightened awareness by the general public on the issues of
food and farming. This newfound interest is what will permanently
change the political landscape and build momentum for the longer-
term tasks of reforming key institutions, rethinking economic strategies, and challenging widely held social values as part of a larger vision
of sustainable agriculture and healthy food systems. The great news is
that there has already been much progress."

MARION KALB

CO-DIRECTOR, NATIONAL FARM TO SCHOOL NETWORK

The network is a program of the Community Food Security Coalition that connects farmers to schools in order to provide healthy, fresh food to children and new markets to farmers.

Marion Kalb has worked diligently for more than twenty-six years, from Los Angeles to Africa, on two quintessential issues—creation of viable markets for farmers and public education about the importance of maintaining and increasing our food production capacity. Without viable markets for selling produce, our farmers will cease operation; and without knowing how important fresh foods are for their diet, or knowing what a truly good ripe peach tastes like, people won't know why they need to support farms. Since the late 1980s Marion has focused on these issues by working on policy at the national level in conjunction with her grassroots networking in various communities.

Besides growing up with food appreciation, Marion's life wake-up call occurred when she traveled to Costa Rica and witnessed the reality of poverty during high school. Disturbed by the lack of access to food, education, and basic life needs, the encounter led her down a path advocating for healthy food and farmers back in the U.S. She pursued a degree in Political Economy at UC Berkeley, fascinated by how corrupt political arrangements tie people to lives of poverty. After her undergraduate degree, she studied "Urban and Rural Planning in Developing Countries" and naturally landed in the Peace Corps, working as an Agricultural Extension Agent in Gabon, Central Africa.

"Peanuts and corn were weighed and sold by the sackful—just basic canvas sacks!" says Marion, remembering the limited resources of the farmers there. Her task was to help the struggling villagers move beyond subsistence living and earn some income from their crops. One effort that was particularly successful was a "market garden," gardens where villagers grew vegetables for Europeans living in the capital city, Libreville, 350 miles away. It was here that Marion developed a "soft spot for farmers as they were at the end of the line in terms of the prices they were given and how they would sell their product," she says. "I really began to respect people who worked really hard for very little remuneration." Upon returning home she continued working for farmers with the Southland Farmers Market Association in Los Angeles during the burgeoning farmers market scene of 1987.

Los Angeles definitely was not known for its farmers markets when Marion started working there, nor were farmers used to selling through the new "formal" market environment. With her extensive knowledge of farming and marketing savvy, Marion became the executive director of the Association, after only two years as a market manager. She kept her position as executive director for twelve years. During this time she was able to pass numerous local and statewide policy measures that improved farmers' viability through the markets, such as passing an ordinance at the county level to allow sampling of foods in the markets in the '90s that was eventually passed by the state.

CONNECTING FARMERS WITH SCHOOLS

"Hot or cold lunch?" the lunch lady asks each child as he or she gets to the front of the line. "Hot lunch" is repeated over and over like a mantra from kindergartners to sixth graders. The choice between the two is painstakingly obvious if you're looking at a cold lunch consisting of a tired salad bar with brown iceberg lettuce, dried-out carrots and a few other unappealing choices. The hot lunch, on the other hand, represents an exciting smorgasbord of fast foods to kids—hamburgers, pizza, burritos, and other microwaveable choices.

School lunch is a perfect example of our dysfunctional food system, and perhaps the most poignant one, as the people who suffer the most are our kids. These fast foods have arisen out of convenience for school districts for a number of reasons—the transition to industrial and centralized kitchens due to population growth and new schools being opened, and a lack of funding to ensure that the offerings at school lunch are healthful and fresh. As school lunch is expected to function as a business within the school, and ideally break even through the sale of school lunches or through federal reimbursements, district school lunch programs do what they have to in order to make the bottom line pencil out. The fresh foods and made-from-scratch meals of the past take more time, labor, and facilities than most schools have available to them. This leaves students who need the meal the most eating junk food.

The farm to school world has been working to reverse this trend and is largely being petitioned by women and concerned parents who want to see their schools offer a healthy environment for learning. Marion has noticed the large involvement of women in the issue: "Children's health, farm marketing, and food service are all fields run largely by women. If you go to a food service–related convention, roughly 90 percent of the participants are women. On top of that, the president of the School Nutrition Association has almost always been female." Women's nurturing roles in children's health and nutrition has led to great improvement and the reinvolvement of farmers with school food service. It was the promised connection with farmers, along with Marion's big heart for farms, that led her to transition away from her work at Southland to work towards providing alternative markets to farmers and healthy food to kids.

Today, as co-director of the National Farm to School Network, Marion advocates for fresh, seasonal food in schools at the Community Food Security Coalition and Center for Food and Justice, a national organization that advocates for increased access to fresh seasonal foods and lobbies for progressive food policy change. Marion's work in the Farm to School Network is to facilitate connections between farmers and school districts, organize and provide assistance to groups across the country interested in implementing farm to school programs, and work on policy issues to increase school districts' capacity to buy direct from farms.

Nearly 30 million children eat school lunch five days a week in the United States.[10] For many, it is their most nutritious meal of the day. Studies show that without the nutrients that come from "real" food, kids can't learn as well. It's as simple as that. A study of students in Appleton, Wisconsin, titled "Better Food, Better Behavior," found that when the Appleton Central Alternative Charter School offered healthy foods including fresh fruits and vegetables and whole grains, the number of disturbances in their classes declined dramatically and their students exhibited improved attention spans.[11]

In our great country of abundant food products, an estimated 20–30 percent of all kids are considered obese, with children of color most at risk for obesity and type II diabetes.[12] These diseases have such adverse health consequences, and it is often posited that these children are not expected to outlive their parents.[13] This alone, perhaps, makes changing school lunch one of the most important battles of our time, determined by the Farm Bill and the Child Reauthorization Act. Each child deserves a chance to learn and have access to healthy foods, especially when it counts the most.

Kids surprise us to no end with what they will and will not eat. If they have learned where a food comes from and how it is grown, chances are they will want to try eating it too. If they get the opportunity to grow it or pick it themselves, it *will* go into their mouths. Many schools have successfully incorporated food-related curriculum into the classroom, and some even plant a school garden or take their classes on farm tours. During these on-farm visits, both the students and school food service departments have the chance to see food as it's being grown, meet farmers, and truly understand the amount of work it takes to grow what we eat.

While the majority of schools don't have the staff to do a lot of prep work on fruits and vegetables, foods like tangerines, small apples, carrots, and broccoli are low-prep alternatives. By working to create solutions to offer these foods within the constraints of our underfunded cafeterias, farmers are able to create alternative markets for products that don't meet conventional produce standards—a win-win situation for kids, farmers, and our future.

FARM TO SCHOOL PROGRAMS IN ACTION

As one of the first school districts in the country to return to fresh, local options for their school food, Santa Monica, California, led the way by implementing a farmers market salad bar that blew their previous school lunch numbers off the charts. Before implementation in 1996, the pilot school for the salad bar had recorded only about ten out of their five hundred students eating from the salad bar on a daily basis. The iceberg lettuce, julienned carrots with a whitish hue, semi-thawed frozen peas, and ranch dressing had (not surprisingly) lost its appeal to students. Collaboration with the Santa Monica Farmers Market—a member of Southland Farmers Market Association that Marion was involved with at the time—helped transition the bar to local and seasonal offerings. The day that it launched, 150 students chose the salad bar. The other good news—besides that kids will eat what they perceive as fresh or good for them—is that the numbers over the years have remained high, with about 125 salad bar meals per day. After the initial success in one school, the food services director took the "Farmers Market Fresh Salad Bar" model to all fifteen of his schools in the district.

That same year, completely separate but synonymous activities were happening in the warm tropical climes of Florida. The New North Florida Cooperative, a group of African American farmers in the Florida panhandle, met with a representative at the USDA to help them access new markets for their foods. The agent facilitated meetings between the group and local school district staff; after a few meetings, the farmers left with a contract for all of their collard greens. This gave the farmers reassurance that they would sell a certain amount to the district and the school district was ensured of a price they could afford. School districts aren't the only food markets to set up contracts; nearly all food service providers do. (Schools are required to "go out to bid" for their food distributor services. In California, these contracts allow up to $50,000 in sales to businesses outside of the contractor, such as farmers.)

WHAT FARM TO SCHOOL PROGRAMS NEED

Farm to school has seen much success over the past thirteen years, synonymous with the growing interest and support of sustainable foods. Currently active in over 40 states, 2,039 school districts and 8,776 schools, the farm to school program is growing annually.[14]

Marion works with a network of leaders in eight different regions of the United States, all representatives of farm to school for their region. This network provides infrastructure to help districts start serving local foods or to advocate for increasing federal dollars to support such programs. Via regional conference calls and a national gathering, which has grown from three hundred to over six hundred attendees since 2000, there are plenty of opportunities for sharing best practices and learning about new developments. "When I started, it was mostly an organizing position," says Marion, "bringing groups together and discussing the challenges to getting more local food into school districts." But soon it became apparent to her that policy would have to change, as federal and state school lunch reimbursements are not high enough to increase fresh and local food offerings. Additionally, as mentioned earlier, farm subsidies contribute to unhealthy junk foods, as less than one percent of subsidies goes toward fresh fruit and vegetable production that is more healthful for students.

Marion feels that for farm to school programs to function well at a national level, we need increased funds for schools through federal funding resources and, at the state level, "the secretaries of Agriculture and Education should be sharing notes and providing each other with lists of school districts and farms," says Marion. Right now there is no consolidated place to access this information. This way, our government agencies would be more interconnected rather than operating in occupational bubbles.

Masked under the very formal name of the Child Nutrition Reauthorization (CNR) Act, this is where the food tray meets the federal budget, and reimbursement rates to schools are determined. CNR comes up every five years for debate and reallocation, just like the Farm Bill. (Its funds cover breakfast, lunch, and after-school snacks.) Marion's organization is currently working on three different levels to create federal policy change for our school's food:

1. Her organization is lobbying to increase the $2.57-per-meal reimbursement rate so that districts have more wiggle room to purchase fresh fruits and vegetables for their students;

2. They're working on creating a competitive grant program to offer startup funds for farm to school programs, so that schools can purchase ovens, cold storage, and other infrastructure;

3. And they're working to help schools to develop seasonal menu planning; procure local products; and develop school gardens.

These funds may also be available to other nonprofit organizations that facilitate the process of increasing a district's ability to serve local and seasonal foods.

The National Farm to School Network is also advocating for an institutional farm to school program within the USDA. This would create an educational arm within the government's existing departments versus having a nonprofit work from outside the bureaucracy assisting farmers in connecting with school districts.

In other words, Marion is trying to work herself out of a job.

RECIPES FOR ACTION

You too can be a policy wonk, farm to school advocate, seed saver, biodiversity enthusiast, or advocate for sustainable food and agriculture. Just start by following your passion, and the rest will fall into place. Below are some ideas. (The Resource section has books, organizations and websites that will help.)

EATER

As an eater, here's how you can plug in:

- Join the organization of your choice that is working on issues you care about and/or sign up for their newsletters. Almost all organizations have them these days. If they don't have a newsletter, find out if you can help create one.
- Support diversity and local producers by eating with the seasons.
- Introduce a friend or family member to the cause of sustainable food by giving them a book from one of the great authors in the Bibliography.
- Start a dialogue with your school about their lunch program. Suggest they try to serve one seasonal, whole piece of fruit to students one time per week. Universities generally have more money and should be incorporating local foods every day.
- Host a film about food at your house, school, or a community venue. The sky is the limit on opportunities to engage food and farming folks at such gatherings.
- Call and write letters to your representatives in support of small farmers, sustainability, and local food (i.e. farm to school programs). By signing up for sustainable food and farming newsletters, you'll get updated about when action is needed.

FARMER

There are always more ways to promote biodiversity on your farm and encourage future generations to know what you grow. You can participate by:

- Working with Seed Savers Exchange or other seed companies to do seed trials.

- Growing/raising heirloom varieties of fruits, vegetables, and animals. At the same time, you might create niche markets.
- Saving your seed.
- Encouraging other farms to cultivate unique varieties.
- Partnering with an organization involved with policy to bring your farmer voice to our representatives.
- Bringing classrooms onto your farm.

FOOD BUSINESS

Diversity of our food depends on the farmer and also on the markets. Businesses can support diversity and sustainability by:

- Buying heirloom varieties of plants and animals.
- Educating the public about unique varieties.
- Supporting direct-marketed local foods.
- Partnering with a farmer and/or community organization to celebrate unique varieties or new seasons in your restaurant.
- Putting your purchasing power to work by buying as diversely and as locally as you can.
- Partnering with a school on their lunch program, doing demos, or sponsoring food events to raise money for a school.

CHAPTER 3

PROMOTING LOCAL & SEASONAL FOOD

When we eat out, we're at the whims and food sourcing preferences of the executive chef. After all, a chef's job includes more than commanding a cadre of employees. Chefs create menus that change seasonally (or that don't) and they have the all-important role of ordering food from various local farmers (or they make only one call to a national distributor).

The average food business makes weekly purchases by calling a mere two or three vendors at the beginning of each week. Bread, toilet paper, linens, fish, onions, apples, dish soap, pan scrubbers, and filet mignon are delivered in one big mass by the big guys such as Aramark, Sysco, and Sodexho. These products arrive, from unknown sources, sometimes every day of the week to accommodate the restaurant industry's voracious food needs and their generally limited storage capacity. As we are a nation of convenience, average food businesses, too, have become accustomed to getting their jobs done as quickly as possible. (For us, it's eating, for them, feeding.) While hopefully by this point in the book we understand the economic benefit of supporting local businesses and farms, we must also realize that buying from more than a few sources is more expensive in prep and administration overhead for food businesses. Someone will have to cover these additional costs—a harsh proposition, as most of us are addicted to cheap foods and their low prices.

As the women in this chapter will tell you, seasonal, sustainable (organic, pesticide-free, transitional), and native (foods endemic to a region) foods outshine any others in flavor and in other benefits of social and environmental responsibility. Additionally, they've found that the joy of diversity, of bringing the seasons' flavors to their customers, and of having relationships with local farms have no monetary value.

Biodiversity of our food is only as diverse as what is on our plates and what eaters demand. According to the Food and Agriculture Organization, "Around ten thousand plant species have been used for human food since the origin of agriculture. Today, only about 150 plant species make up the diets of the majority of the world's population."[1] A group of seven organizations found the loss of biodiversity in our diets disconcerting enough that they've formed a coalition called Renewing America's Food Traditions (RAFT), which works to resuscitate our dwindling edible species. These foods, the very fabric of our history and food culture, have outstanding personalities and are summed up well in Deborah Madison's foreword for the book *Renewing America's Food Traditions:*

Many of these [RAFT] foods bear colorful names. I especially like the Waldoboro Green Neck turnip, the Death Valley devil's claw, and the Pike's Peak squash. And all of them come with stories—stories of origin as well as tales of near disappearance and, sometimes, almost miraculous reappearance. These stories make you want to connect, to bring these foods literally into your own life, and in many cases we can do that. But not all of these RAFT foods are still with us today. Some, like the passenger pigeon, are fully extinct, while others teeter on the brink: white abalone, leatherback sea turtle, goliath grouper, Cotton Patch goose, and masked bobwhite quail, to name a few. They are emblematic of the misfortune that falls on a food.

At the other extreme, though, are RAFT foods that, with little more than a trip to the Web and maybe a phone call, we can find ourselves feasting on: hand-parched wild rice, Santa Maria pinquito beans, Narragansett turkeys, Pixie tangerines, Sierra Beauty apples, and Black Sphinx dates.

And while farmers with that knowledge are passing onto greener pastures, so too have fruit and vegetable varieties dwindled due to a lack of proliferating such varieties through mainstream distribution channels. According to RAFT, we are down to fifteen hundred varieties of apples from fifteen thousand a century ago. Gone are some of the flavors that compelled us into cultivating the *Malus* species—tart and tangy, sweet and crunchy, dry sauvignon, and a multitude of combinations to match every taste.[2] The same scenario appears when it comes to peaches and any other fruit or vegetable you can find in your produce department. There are hundreds of varieties of peaches (not just yellow and white) and hundreds of varieties in the leguminosae (bean), rutacea (citrus), and solanaceae (nightshade, tomato) families. Next time you're in a grocery store, count the astonishing few varieties you see—varieties that are most often selected for their long storage life and not for their spectacular aroma and flavor.

The chefs, food writers, and food researchers featured in this chapter are working to transform the delicious gifts from the fields and bring them back to our palates. They lead us with their spirit of celebration, education, and enjoyment while supporting our food traditions and family farmers around the country.

DEBORAH MADISON

AUTHOR AND CHEF

In 2002, before the craze of local foods really took off, Deborah Madison brought out a portrait of America's regional foods based on her years of visiting one hundred farmers markets from Hawaii to Maine, capturing the essence of farmers and their food in hot and cold climes alike. The outcome of her adventure was manifested in *Local Flavors: Cooking and Eating From America's Farmers Markets*. Delighting her readers with seasonal recipes, priceless anecdotes, food lore, and market profiles, she brings them along to the best places to find food diversity across the United States.

Her original vision was to chart out the seasonality of the entire country on a twelve-month cycle. But she decided in the end that she "didn't want to make it place-based [specific to different regions] as the issues of local food apply to everyone no matter where they were." She points out that it would have required *thousands* of charts for each micro-climate, one for every one thousand feet in elevation, a task that maybe technology will be able to do one day.

Deborah has long been a leader of local food and flavor, starting over thirty years ago on her mission to make vegetarian cooking delicious, which she accomplished through opening Greens Restaurant in San Francisco. Today she is finding that "people really get the book [*Local Flavors*] now as they better understand 'local food and farms.'" The recent growth of farmers markets in the country is a testament to such support, and the book is in its second edition.

But Deborah also sees that we have a long way to go. "My experience through that particular conduit of farmers markets would tell me that it has changed and come into focus for a lot of people. I'm not always sure what 'local' means to people. It could be like the word 'sustainable.' However, when you get down to it, the whole issue of purveying local foods is that it takes a lot of commitment and work. It's easy in the summer—you can go to a farmers market and get a lot of fruits and vegetables—but to go beyond that and to look at meat and dairy, to support the effort and pay the prices, to grow some food of your own, is another level of challenge."

"In season is where you live—you can't separate season from place."

Regardless of the challenges inherent in being a "locavore," Deborah remains optimistic. "People *are* starting to get it. I was at our market in December and it was snowing out. There was a gentleman from out of town that said, 'I wish I could get some strawberries right now, but I guess they aren't in season.' He actually realized that they were out of season, and that's a pretty big step for many people."

CONNECTING TO FOOD THROUGH KNOWING ITS STORIES

"When we eat, we do so much more than put food in our mouths," says Deborah, knowing that behind every meal is a long line of hands that help the food transition from fields to our plates. "We've lived for so long without a story—without any idea of where our food comes from, how it's raised, and who the people are that grow and produce it—that we have become out of touch with our food."

At farmers markets, the smell of fresh foods, the irregular shaped vegetables and fruits, and the surprises found on tables toppling with abundance brings not only the opportunity to hunt for your dinner, but also to smell the earth and see the vibrancy of life picked only the day before. The markets allow us to tap into our primal hunter-gatherer urges, which can bring us to sensory overload as we breathe in a fresh peach or just-baked bread, or sample homemade cheese. For Deborah, the farmers market experience holds the key to the vibrant food economy of the future, saying, "Food comes from some place, not someplace else." In comparison, chain supermarkets stock foods based on length of shelf life. Fruits and vegetables are picked before they are ripe and are covered in wax, making it really difficult to smell the produce and know whether it is ripe before buying it. The other food departments—dairy, meat, bakery, and others—have analogous stories. *Seasonal* literally means *local* since you can't ship ripe foods without them being damaged. "In season is where you live," says Deborah.

"You can't separate season from place. The supermarket represents the season of the world. The farmers market is the season of *your* world."

CREATIVE SEASONAL COOKING

Growing up, Deborah learned to bake from her mother and gained an appreciation of hearty Midwestern food from her father. The family had a big vegetable garden and many fruit trees, so to Deborah, "eating locally in summer is nothing new." Her father tested her palate with new and exciting foods such as kumquats and quince, which largely influenced her ease in the kitchen.

As an advocate for family farmers and food diversity, Deborah learned her seasonal sensibilities on farmland just outside of Davis, California. As a student of Buddhism, a chef in San Francisco, and through her years working as a farmers market manager in Santa Fe, she brings her passion to the rest of us through her writings, which have earned both prestigious James Beard and International Association of Culinary Professionals book awards. From *Vegetarian Cooking for Everyone* to *Local Flavors,* Deborah has been inspiring her readers to take the fate of their food into their own hands since the 1980s.

As a conscientious omnivore, Deborah was drawn into food through vegetarian cooking in the late 1960s at the San Francisco Zen Center. It was here that she would find a new respect for the simplistic beauty and flavors of vegetables. Meat wasn't central to her diet at the Zen Center (not allowed), nor did meat play a big role in her diet while growing up, so the transition to vegetarian eating and cooking was an easy one. Besides not having a strong affinity to animal protein, she remembers the first time she saw the film *Meat* in the 1970s. The film showed the inner workings of our modern-day industrial meat packing plants. "It was utterly shocking and compelling," she says. "I knew then that I didn't want to participate in that type of food system. Ever." She still holds firm that the industrialized food system, particularly that which produces meat, is one that she refuses to participate in.

While at the Zen Center, Deborah took on the role of creating vegetarian meals with gusto, and she added life to previously unimaginative dishes that were served for breakfast, lunch, and dinner. This made her a natural fit to help the Zen Center open Greens Restaurant—the first gourmet vegetarian restaurant—in San Francisco in 1979. Deborah was there from the start, cooking up vegetables from the Zen Center's affiliated Marin County farm, Green Gulch, where she lived for many years. Aside from teaching Zen students how to chop, slice and dice, she and gardener Wendy Johnson experimented with the new varieties of seeds Deborah brought back from France while on a trips: arugula, four-season lettuce, and borage, new on the food scene at the time. Deborah and Wendy, while both living there, would enjoy each other's company in their parallel universes of "slightly controlled chaos"—one in the fields and the other in the kitchen. Deborah recalls how she would create her menus in her head in the twenty-five minutes from the farm to the restaurant—a sign of a true chef. She used whatever ingredient she could from Green Gulch, and she set up various accounts with farms in the Suisun Valley and other areas that could grow hot-weather crops not grown on the coastal climes of Marin.

"FARMING IS A DEEP ART"

Growing up with a botanist father aided in the development of Deborah's commitment to promoting and preserving food biodiversity. Knowing the plants by name, growing up surrounded by walnut orchards, and swimming in the irrigation canals created a special place in her heart for our rural working spaces. Her brother, Mike Madison, also took root in farming. Today, he farms not far from where they grew up, and he grows a variety of melons, apricots, vegetables and beautiful bundled flowers that he sells with his wife at the Davis Farmers Market. He makes some of the finest hand-pressed olive oil from his olive orchard in Yolo County, where olive trees are going in faster than grapes. As a first generation farmer, Mike has learned the ups (great dinners and harvest years) and downs (gophers and late freezes) that farming as a lifestyle affords. What he and Deborah have both learned through their upbringing in addition to their appreciation of seasonal foods is that the knowledge base needed to farm is not easy to come by these days.

"I'm looking for people who really understand fruit, farmers who really go into their art. In general, people aren't really specialized today," she says. "There isn't that kind of Jeffersonian agrarian wisdom that used to exist in the United States. Farming is a deep art." We need multi-generational farmers around to answer the questions the new crop of farmers have about growing their heirloom varieties. What soils do its roots prefer? Which plants, when located together, protect each other from insects and disease? The age-old traditions and knowledge handed down from generation-to-generation have been waning just as the varieties we eat have diminished.

In our stores there is another kind of information gap she has noticed. "You see plums—black plums and red plums," says Deborah. "You might not know there are hundreds of varieties in all colors—purple, green, yellow, blue." She knows that this is in part due to the buyers who are limiting our options by carrying only those fruits suited for travel. However, outside of the supermarket, this trend is starting to reverse as old varieties are again coming back by the virtue of increasing eater demand for local foods and good flavors.

> Old varieties are again coming back by the virtue of increasing eater demand for local foods and good flavors.

"Consumers should be able to say, 'This is a Blenheim, this is a Royal, this is a Katy. These are great for eating fresh; these for canning and pies; what you're looking for in an apricot are the speckles; these are better dried,'" says Deborah.

LOCAL AS A LIFESTYLE

Deborah herself has taken on the challenge of growing food at home. After installing eight raised vegetable beds at her house, she says, "The experience of growing food for yourself is humbling, bewildering and, at times, downright frustrating! A lot of people want gardens, but they don't necessarily want to garden." While the armchair gardener envisions perfectly manicured beds full of organic vegetables, fruits, and healthy soils, the reality is that "it's really hard work," says Deborah, "at least here in New Mexico where our skills are constantly tested by poor soil and bad weather." And she's not even out among her rows of chard, lettuces, tomatoes, and peppers every day or even every weekend. She realizes there is a big learning curve that starts with seasonality and flavor and that may, eventually, lead to the garden.

"Taking on gardening is especially daunting for people that haven't done that for generations. There's so much more to learn than most of us imagine." But according to Deborah, encouraging home gardens is a vital component to bridging the gap of awareness and sensitivity to food culture. "Otherwise it seems that we're talking agribusiness food as the food people can afford and farmers market food as what people can't afford—as if there's nothing in between. Neither model emphasizes self-sufficiency as that *is* something in between." It's often said that we do not preserve what we do not understand, but we would do well to try. Gardening is the closest we get to observing all the seasonal cycles and gaining a deeper appreciation of a farmer's work.

At her home in New Mexico, Deborah continues cooking, publishing, and promoting local flavors to help bring back a more sensible food culture for the United States. She serves on the board of the Seed Savers Exchange, which promotes seed saving and trading among America's gardeners. She is also active with Slow Food and Renewing America's Food Traditions (RAFT), organizations built on preserving and encouraging appreciation in heirloom foods and conviviality. She accomplishes this as a freelance writer and as a consultant. (One of her recent consulting projects was to create menus for Berkeley's CAL Dining Services.) To get people back in the kitchen, she and her husband, Patrick McFarlin, wrote a book called *What We Eat When We Eat Alone*. Deborah's contributions continue to inspire present and future generations to know their food, to meet a farmer at a market, and to try gardening and cooking for themselves.

JESSICA PRENTICE

AUTHOR, CHEF AND CO-OWNER, THREE STONE HEARTH

Three Stone Hearth is a cooperative food business that creates meals that people can take home, using local ingredients.

Point Reyes Books in West Marin, California, is a place where people meet, talk, simmer, get inspired, and ferment ideas. And it was the very location where "locavores" was hatched in 2005. Jessica Prentice and Sage Van Wing knew each other from farmers markets, but it was here at the bookstore that Sage pitched the idea to Jessica of challenging people to eat foods grown within a one-hundred-mile radius for an entire month. At the time, Jessica was in the process of finishing up her book *Full Moon Feast* at the Mesa Refuge, a writers' retreat just outside Point Reyes Station, and often walked to the bookstore for inspiration and a chat. Sage and Jessica's walking distance from the shore. These discussions eventually inspired the "foodshed for thought" challenge by Sage, and brought Jessica together with two of Sage's cohorts to birth a national movement—the Locavores.

But the word "locavore" wouldn't come until later. It emerged from a tight deadline at the *San Francisco Chronicle* inspired by World Environment Day, a day when one hundred mayors convened in San Francisco to discuss climate change and greening their cities. Sage's press release about "foodshed for thought" (the name they used before Locavores was invented) had reached the desk of reporter Olivia Wu. Olivia found it a good tie-in with the summit and food aspirations that San Francisco is known for. She decided to write a story on this one-hundred-mile challenge.

Weeks before writing the article, Olivia needed to taste it to believe it. Following Jessica around Berkeley's Tuesday farmers market, she was able to capture the procurement of a locally grown meal first hand. June at the market offered an astounding variety: radishes, snap peas, ground wheat, rice, almonds, and loads of various fruits. After the market experience, Jessica settled into her home kitchen to make Olivia a simple, outstanding "locavore" meal of homemade mashed potatoes with raw cream from Claravale Farm, snap peas from Full Belly Farm with mint picked from Jessica's yard, and locally raised pork chops brined for two days before frying.

Jessica was on the phone with Olivia a few days after their dinner when Olivia asked, "What are you calling yourselves?" "I don't know," Jessica said. "I can't call it 'Foodshed for Thought.' You have until five o'clock to think of a name," Olivia said.

The question echoed in Jessica's head. A quick call to Sage got nothing but voicemail—so Jessica was on her own. Luckily for her, one of her favorite things (besides food, of course) is digging into word etymologies. "I brainstormed and wrote down 'local eaters' . . . 'women who eat locally,' and then went online and looked up the Greek and Latin for 'to eat' and 'local.' In Greek, 'to eat' is *phage,* like esophagus—a pretty ugly word." She kept thinking. "Carnivore, omnivore, herbivore. *Vorare* is the Latin root for 'to swallow,' 'to devour,' 'voracious.' So that was nice. *Local* comes from the Latin root of 'locus,' meaning 'place.'" (*Loca* also means "crazy" in Spanish, but Jessica thought, "Who cares if people think we're crazy?!") She managed to email Olivia with the idea thirty minutes before her deadline. "How about 'The Locavores?'" she wrote. Olivia responded with two words: "Love it."

Olivia Wu wrote on June 1, 2005, "Calling themselves the Locavores, the women—Lia McKinney, Jessica Prentice, Dede Sampson and Sage Van Wing—are passionate about eating locally and have devised a way to show others how to do that . . . " The story made the front page of the *San Francisco Chronicle*'s food section, and the movement was on.

In August of that year the group promoted their first Eat Local Challenge, a now annual event that challenges the taste buds and sourcing capacities for those living in California and around the country. This has since caught on with other food communities, including institutions and restaurants still experimenting with the one-hundred-mile diet. Chefs Collaborative, a consortium of chefs from around the country that prioritize sustainability, has contributed to its popularity. But perhaps the biggest keystone moment happened in 2007 when the *New Oxford American Dictionary* chose "locavore" as the Word of the Year.

COMMUNITY SUPPORTED KITCHENS

Before "locavore" got traction, Jessica was already thinking of her next innovative plan to combine food, business, and community. Having been self-employed for two years, she had acquired a multitude of skills, from marketing to bookkeeping. Jessica wanted to find a way to incorporate her skills of chefing and nutrition in a business model that wasn't so taxing. "I have strengths and weaknesses [in business] and needed to partner with other people if I wanted to have a business that will make up for those weaknesses and create more balance," she says.

It was around this time that she received an email from out in cyberspace (on a listserve) asking: "Is anyone out there doing a community supported kitchen?" That's how she first met Margo Baldwin (who would later become her publisher at Chelsea Green). "Before that, I had never heard anyone else use that term," says Jessica, although she had been chewing over that very same idea for years. The concept would come to mean a kitchen that has community shares or investors, just like a farmer-run CSA.

A few years later, that initial brainstorm for an alternative business model was birthed into Three Stone Hearth, the worker-owned cooperative that Jessica co-founded with four other worker-owners (Larry Wisch, Catherine Spanger, Misa Koketsu, and Porsche Combash). "We wanted to implement a business model where we get paid a reasonable wage for doing something that is valuable and makes a contribution to our community." Their model is shaped by values of community, sustainability, and profitability, as Three Stone Hearth creates meals that people can take home, "not necessarily to *supplant* dinner," says Jessica, "but more along the lines of *supplement*. My big concern was to not feed into the world of convenience foods and people not cooking, but I really think there are some people who are not going to cook, period. And for others, having a few things that are prepared actually moves them back into the kitchen."

An array of these helpful additions include broths, soups, stews, baked pies, lacto-fermented vegetables like sauerkraut, beverages like kombucha, sourdough crackers, artisanal cold cereals, patés, and pastured meat patties. In addition to getting people back in the kitchen,

Jessica's book, *Full Moon Feast,* helps break down traditional and indigenous processing techniques to help people move into doing more on their own. Admittedly, Jessica knows that "once you learn about traditional processing techniques and approaches to preparation of food, it can make cooking even more intimidating. For example, traditional peoples ate freshly ground or whole grains that were sprouted, soaked, soured, or leavened before being baked or cooked. Once you understand how much more digestible and nourishing grains can be if you approach them that way, it's hard not to follow suit. But it's also a whole new ball game in terms of cooking. It takes a lot more time, energy, expertise and experience to work with grains that way." But Three Stone Hearth is not just about offering people these more nutritious foods or making them more convenient, it is also about the potential efficiencies of making them on a community scale—such as making forty gallons of soup or a thirty-liter crock of sauerkraut and then dividing it up into returnable mason jars. (Cooking and prepping in bulk is more energetically and economically efficient than making smaller batches.)

"We wanted to implement a business model where we get paid a reasonable wage for doing something that is valuable and makes a contribution to our community."

Three Stone Hearth is an evolution of the farm-based CSA model that is connected not only to community but to culture and tradition as well. In *Full Moon Feast,* Jessica articulates this perspective by connecting our eating seasons to traditional moon phases and offering an interesting perspective on various foods that were once part of our diet and those that continue on as mainstays in other cultures. These values are integral to Three Stone Hearth, where the very name comes from the centrality that the hearth plays in the home and the community. As their website explains: "The Three Stone Hearth is a reminder that cooking and food have been central to community life throughout human history, and that when we prepare food we are engaging in a fundamental, universal, and profoundly meaningful human activity."

Jessica's awareness helped form this community supported business model that perhaps others will be inspired to adopt. "Our food system is not only factory farmed but it's also factory processed," says Jessica. "So much of what we eat is from factories. One of the reasons I got involved in local foods—one of the things that is most important to me—is *relationships* versus *anonymity*. My deep frustration, and even grief, is that our food system is so *anonymous*." She emphasizes the fact that we so rarely know the source, the farmer, the place, or anything about the story of our food. Going to the store is an impersonal experience too. Jessica points out that there is no transparency in a grocery store and that "advertising is designed to try to give a sense of relationship that is missing. . . . You put the little characters on the food so that people can feel connected to it, or a bucolic image or a familiar face, so when you're eating that thing, you think you're connected somehow. It's just this *illusion* of connection. But there really is a way to reconnect to the people and places where our food comes from, and that's the big underlying theme with all of my work—how to make the connection.

"In the long run people will see that eating locally is just common sense. Eventually," says Jessica, "that apple from New Zealand is going to stop being cheaper than an apple that's grown an hour away from here. The prices will start to even out. When that happens, people will start valuing their apple trees again and start seeing their food as the precious thing that it is."

She points out that we don't really understand the value of our ecological systems and food is at the basis of this. "If we care about our local ecosystems and our local economies, we have to be willing to make real food a priority. . . . People kick and scream, saying that local or organic foods are too expensive. But what about cell phones, cable television, fancy cosmetics and all these *other* things that we spend tons of money on in this country? Paying $2.50 per pound for peaches is branded 'elitist,' but for some reason paying $250 for tennis shoes is not. Why? I would argue that food is something that is completely essential and these other things aren't. They're optional." This is where her business comes in. She's able to buy direct from local farms, educate her customers, and create a new economic reality based on the type of food system she envisions—one that is appreciated, local, sustainable, and healthful.

JUDY WICKS

AUTHOR AND RESTAURATEUR, WHITE DOG CAFÉ

White Dog Café is a restaurant that sources fresh, local, humanely raised foods.

FOUNDER, WHITE DOG COMMUNITY ENTERPRISES

White Dog Community Enterprises' mission is to build a more equitable food system and local economy for the Philadelphia region.

Outside of the White Dog Café, an energy emanates. A group of contented folks spill out onto the street after a community storytelling event and a meal that filled their bellies with locally sourced American comfort foods. Since the White Dog Café's opening in 1983, this scene has repeated itself again and again. As one of the most widely known small business advocates and restaurant owners in the country, owner Judy Wicks has spent the past few decades in an open dialogue with the public about a new business model that builds community and creates self-reliance, beginning with sustainable local food systems. She's been so successful at this conversation that she launched the restaurant's nonprofit beneficiary, White Dog Community Enterprises, and a national nonprofit organization, the Business Alliance for Local Living Economies (BALLE), to expand this message beyond her 19104 zip code.

While growing up north of Pittsburgh in the small town of Ingomar, some of Judy's earliest memories with local food and community were at home. She picked fresh vegetables from her parent's garden and witnessed the "Hungry Club," a potluck dinner party that her parents participated in one Friday a month with their longtime friends. It's somewhat surprising that she went into the restaurant industry at all, considering that at an early age she rejected the gender role of cooking and food preparation entirely. Despite the encouragement of her food-savvy mother and grandmother, who gardened, preserved, and cooked, Judy rebelled. "I refused to learn to cook because my hobby was to build cabins in the woods," she remembers. "I really hated anything to do with cooking or sewing and felt distraught that girls were expected to learn these skills versus doing things that they truly wanted to do. Like carpentry."

During her post-college experience as a VISTA volunteer in an Alaskan Eskimo village with her husband, she witnessed an indigenous lifestyle, food culture, and craftsmanship that led to a cultural awakening. Unlike the consumer society she grew up in, Eskimo culture rejected materialism, sharing everything with their neighbors and never accumulating more than they needed. From this experience, Judy began to envision a new economy, one based on cooperation rather than competition, and on sharing, rather than hoarding.

After their return from Alaska, Judy and her husband tried to figure out what to do next. "In 1970, I suggested we open a store, because I had spent a little time making things when I was little and selling them from my wagon. The business we opened, which we called the Free People's Store, has gone on to be really successful and has also birthed Urban Outfitters today," she says nonchalantly. At the time, she and her husband were living in the store as they couldn't afford the rent on both retail space and an apartment. "After about a year into running the store, I decided I had to leave my husband and find my own way. I packed my bags and took off. I was only a half-block from the store, when I went through a red light and got in an accident. No one was hurt, thankfully," says Judy. When a man asked if he could walk her home she replied, "I'm not going home. I just left my husband, and now my car is wrecked, so I have to get a job immediately." The man said that he worked for a French restaurant that he knew needed a waitress, and Judy said, "I'll take it! To this day, when anyone asks me how I got in the restaurant industry I always say, 'by accident,'" she laughs.

After Judy had been waitressing at LaTerrasse for two years (and writing a book at the same time), the owner, absentee and living in Boston, came down to find his business in disarray. He fired the manager and gave the job to Judy that same afternoon. Walking out the door, he said it would only be for the interim. "So there I was with fifty employees in a one-hundred-seat restaurant, just promoted from waitress to manager. I started doing some common sense things, like cleaning out the basement and writing job descriptions for everyone," she says.

Despite the owner telling her that it would be temporary, Judy ended up managing the restaurant for ten years. "Over time I became quite successful at it, and that's when I realized that the restaurant could be used as a vehicle for social change. That's really been my interest more than anything. Even before I was in the food movement I could see that gathering people around food was a way to organize and bring about social change."

> "Even before I was in the food movement, I could see that gathering people around food was a way to organize and bring about social change."

Judy left LaTerrasse in 1983 and opened the White Dog Café just down the street, with a mission of "serving customers, community, employees, and the natural environment." She created numerous community-building and educational programs that focus on sustainable agriculture, social and economic justice, and community arts. Infused and passionate about world peace and human rights, she started an international "sister restaurant" project to educate customers about the effects of U.S. foreign policy on the lives of people in other countries. By organizing trips to countries in political conflict with the United States, Judy worked toward her dream that through education and by listening to others' perspectives, citizens could move U.S. policy from one of economic and military domination to one based on a more cooperative economic system. Essentially fair trade. Matching this passion with commerce, Judy opened the Black Cat adjacent to the restaurant. This gift store carried fairly traded goods and, along with the White Dog, exemplified the cooperative and sustainable economic system that she envisioned.

FOOD AS SOCIAL CHANGE

At the White Dog Café, Judy shifted course away from her previous culinary experience at LaTerrasse to focus the menu on American foods, similar to the cuisine her parents served at the Hungry Club. She was excited to get away from "all that French food," with the heavy cream sauces and imported ingredients. Wanting the menu to bring nutrition and simplicity to people's lives, she hired a chef with a style based on fresh, local ingredients. "We were already doing pasture-raised chickens and cage-free eggs when I read John Robbins' *Diet for a New America*." This book was an exposé on animal cruelty, and it also discussed environmentalism and the benefits of a more plant-based diet. It drastically changed her outlook on how her business needed to become more conscious of the wellbeing of farm animals.

"When I found out about the plight of pigs in factory farms," she says, "and realized that the pork I had been serving at the White Dog came from a horrendous system with such abuse to the animals and pollution to the environment, I went in the kitchen and told them to take all of the pork off the menu—bacon, pork chops, ham, all of it-until we could find a humane source." Judy asked the farmer selling them free-range chicken and eggs if he knew a farm that raised pigs on pasture, and eventually found a farmer from Lancaster County to supply her with two pigs per week. Making the transition from receiving three specific cuts—bacon, chops, and ham—to an entire animal is quite the process for a restaurant to undertake. The menu would need to change, oftentimes daily, in order to make use of the whole animal.

The restaurant's local and humane meat sourcing kept evolving as she learned about the "plight of the cow" and "the plight of the sea creatures." Judy kept digging deeper into the sourcing of her ingredients until, before she knew it, she had humanely and sustainably sourced the entire menu of the White Dog with foods that meshed with her community and environmental values. (This included serving organic fresh fruits and vegetables whenever possible, sustainable seafood, and fairly traded imported items such as coffee, chocolate, and teas.) After all this work she said, "I'm finished now—the menu is cruelty-free and comes from humane sources, and this can be a market niche for the White Dog. But then," she says, "I realized that it wasn't enough to have one restaurant buying from local farmers. And if I really cared about the animals, the environment, the workers, the farmers, and the consumers that ate the meat, then rather than keep this as my market niche, I should share this information with my competitors."

This realization was a real turning point for Judy and her career. She moved from being a competitive businessperson to sharing her sources and practices openly with other businesses—embodying the spirit of the Inuit culture she experienced so many years ago. She realized that cooperation among businesses was critical to building a more humane and environmentally sustainable food system.

With a clear vision, she took off. In 2001 Judy started the White Dog Café Foundation (later called White Dog Community Enterprises), her 501c(3) to which she dedicated 20 percent of her pre-tax proceeds. This nonprofit would house the Fair Food Project, which was created to educate restaurants on how to buy from farmers, and the public on how to buy locally.

When the foundation first began their restaurant outreach to realize Judy's vision of sharing her knowledge, Judy talked to her pork distributor to find out what it would take for him to meet the demand of the new markets they were helping create. His big need was a refrigerated truck to transport more pork to restaurants—so Judy lent him the $30,000. Fair Food has prospered over the years and now runs a dizzying array of programs that foster more vibrant rural communities and farms, including Buy Fresh Buy Local, Farm to Institution, and the Fair Food Farmstand. With the wheels in motion, Judy refocused her energies on an even bigger vision of impacting not just the food businesses of her community, but to extend her activities to impact the vibrancy of locally owned and operated businesses around the country.

In 1999, two events caused Judy to begin her nationally oriented work. The first was the protest against the World Trade Organization (WTO) in Seattle, and her perceived need for a well-articulated alternative vision to corporate globalization. She saw people protesting what they didn't want in the world—primarily corporate control of food and government—but what were the alternatives? The second event was the forced buyout of Ben & Jerry's by a multinational corporation. Seeing a leading company in the responsible business movement sell out to a larger corporation raised an alarm about the increasing concentration of wealth and power in the economy. In fall of 2001, Judy co-founded the Business Alliance with Local Living Economies (BALLE), along with Laury Hammel (who had co-founded Business for Social Responsibility in 1991). Judy and Laury met while serving on the board of the Social Venture Network (SVN), an organization composed of social entrepreneurs and investors. BALLE was started as a program of SVN and eventually spun off as its own organization. Earlier that same year, Judy founded the Sustainable Business Network of Greater Philadelphia (SBN) in her home community, which became a charter member of BALLE.

> Judy's mission for change and counterintuitive approach to business boils down to attaining social and environmental justice through cooperation.

The formation of BALLE firmly planted Judy's stake in the ground for revitalizing America's small businesses and family farmers. Her bold mission for change and counterintuitive approach to business boils down to attaining social and environmental justice through cooperation. Since the organization was launched, more than seventy-five chapters are now active across the country and in Canada. In order to focus full time on the local living economy movement, Judy sold the White Dog Café in January of 2009. In her unique exit strategy, she retains ownership of the name "White Dog Café" and licenses it back to the new owners along with a social contract. The contract lists the business practices that must be adhered to in order to conduct business under the name. By including such practices as sourcing from local farmers, and serving only humanely raised animal products, sustainably sourced fish and seafood, and fairly traded—imported ingredients, Judy's values live on as a model for others.

The ongoing success of the White Dog Café demonstrates that "doing good" as a business can also do good for people and the earth.

Protecting What We Love
by Judy Wicks

(printed with permission by Judy Wicks)

At its heart, our movement for local living economies is about love.

And it is love that can overcome the fear that many may feel in the hard days ahead brought on by climate change and environmental collapse. In my own experience, it was my love for animals that motivated me to challenge the factory farm system and begin building a local living economy in my region.

Our power comes from protecting what we love—love of place, love of life—people, animals, nature, all of life on our beautiful planet Earth. And I would say, for the entrepreneurs amongst us, it's also about a love of business. Business has been corrupted as an instrument of greed rather than one of service to the common good. Yet we know that business is beautiful when we put our creativity and care into producing a product or service needed by our community.

Our materialistic society has desensitized us to the suffering that underlies our industrial economic system. We're also desensitized by a false idea of masculinity based on control and domination. We need a more feminine, nurturing approach to life to bring forth the goddess in each of us, men and women both, bringing care and compassion to our economy, and peace and harmony to our world.

We must open our hearts and eyes and ears—to hear the cry of the pigs in the crates, of a cow for her calf, of animals in laboratories, in the fur industry.

To feel the suffering of men, women, and children enslaved in sweatshops, in the rug industry, in diamond and coal mines, and in chocolate production. The suffering of migrant workers in slaughterhouses and pesticide-soaked industrial farms. The suffering of the people of Iraq, of Nigeria, of the rainforest tribes—everywhere where there is oil and natural resources to exploit and fight wars over.

Let us hear the cry of the whales, of the polar bears, of the trees, of the coral reefs, of the whole natural world that is dying around us.

What provides the energy and passion for all we must do in this movement is simply to love and protect what we truly care about. And in so doing, find our place as humans in the family of life.

TRACI MILLER

RESTAURATEUR, L'ETOILE

L'Etoile is a restaurant that sources local, fresh, seasonal ingredients in Madison, Wisconsin.

Traci Miller and her brother, Tory, grew up working in their grandparent's diner in Racine, Wisconsin, serving delicious burgers and house-made root beer. At a young age Traci and Tory were already a natural team, with Traci diving into front-of-the-house hospitality and Tory eagerly working the grill in the back of the house. Throughout their childhood Traci and Tory not only gained a flair for hospitality; they also gained the knowledge that comes from growing up on a farm. Growing their own vegetables, picking berries, and working with animals all developed their appreciation for a farm's bounty and for the intense flavors really fresh ingredients can offer. These childhood experiences became invaluable to the siblings when they went into business together some fifteen years later, in May of 2005, to take on the L'Etoile restaurant in Madison, Wisconsin.

Traci's path back into the restaurant world would be circuitous. She studied pharmacy and worked for nine years as a hospital pharmacist, as well as thirteen months as a volunteer pharmacist for Mercy Ships in West Africa, before Tory approached her about the restaurant. Tory, on the other hand, knew he wanted to get back into the kitchen while still in college, so he left his chemistry studies to pursue a professional career at the French Culinary Institute. Tory worked in several high-end New York kitchens before returning to Wisconsin to work with Odessa Piper the founder of L'Etoile. Traci, a long-time professional pharmacist at this point, was in Paris at a friend's wedding when she received the call.

"I have two partners lined up to purchase L'Etoile with me," Tory spoke excitedly on the other end of the line. After hearing her brother's enthusiasm, Traci replied, "I would feel much more comfortable if I handled the business portion for you myself," instead of Tory working with two already established business partners. She knew that even though the business partners lived in Minneapolis, they would have the power to outvote Tory in decision-making. Tory called back the next day just to make sure she was serious.

While Traci's pharmacy career was very successful, she was intrigued by the opportunity to work with her brother. "Although I enjoyed being a pharmacist, I didn't experience the passion for my profession that Tory does. One of the things that attracted me to the L'Etoile venture was the opportunity to be around a person who was realizing his dream every day. That is so addictive when you're in the middle of it." So from this point on, they reverted back to their childhood roles, with Tory managing the food, purchasing, and menus, and Traci handling the front of the house and the business affairs.

Traci describes the process of coming into the restaurant as "quite the learning curve! It's really hard to explain what we do to another restaurateur. Where they might have twenty to twenty-five checks per month to write to their different suppliers, here we have so many farms that we buy directly from, it's a full time job just writing checks," she says. And while it might be a "cumbersome process," she realizes how rewarding it is to be tied that closely to their food community. "The fruits of that labor are amazing and worth doing ten times over," she says.

The exhaustive list of farmers that L'Etoile buys from throughout the year shows a dedication difficult to match, especially in comparative northern climates such as those found in Madison. With a winter wind chill factor at 20 degrees below zero on some days, it's hard to imagine getting anything fresh at all. However, the restaurant manages beautifully with all of their put-by produce, hoop-house spinach and cellared root crops, available through their network of local farms. Honey, jams and jellies, sustainable meats and fish, artisan cheeses and dairy products, and various nuts are also available throughout the year to round out the menu. Come summer, the bountiful growing season brings back blueberries, strawberries, cherries, apples, salad greens, carrots, kales, and much more.

What she didn't know going in was that their business would be as seasonal as their ingredients. "It took me an entire year to understand what the ebbs and flows are financially. May is the biggest month, when everything should be paid off from the winter and it's time to begin saving for the next winter season. You have to plan for three months of down time." While people still venture out on frigid winter evenings for dinner in Madison, business doesn't compare to summertime, when the farmers market is booming across the street. The market, touted as the largest producer-only farmers market in the country, wraps around the capitol with over 150 vendors coming to the square every Saturday from April until November. L'Etoile is right on the square in the middle of all the action and greatly benefits from the proximity.

Traci and Tory have a vigorous passion for local food sources, expanding the foundation built by the restaurant's founder, Odessa Piper. Odessa undeniably led the Midwest momentum for local food purchasing starting with L'Etoile's opening in 1976. "In those very early years the first regular supplier was my older sister Kathleen Piper," says Odessa. "She had a small farm near where I had started out farming in Rolling Ground, Wisconsin. Kathleen had a *massive* vegetable garden, chickens, and goats and regularly came into town to wait tables to make ends meet. I was able to procure a lot of wild gathered foods from her as well." The Dane County Farmers Market was just getting going when L'Etoile was founded, and one of the first farmers Odessa started buying from was Mrs. Meinholtz, "who sold vegetables, beautiful fresh eggs and hickory nuts that her husband hand cracked. Her daughter, Mary Ellen, still sells to the restaurant today," says Odessa.

To add to their local offerings, Tory and Traci opened Café Soleil in October of 2005, downstairs from L'Etoile. In this more casual setting, they serve sustainable and locally grown meats, cheeses, vegetables, in-house baked breads and pastries, coffee and espresso from Just Coffee (a local Madison roaster) and other local fare. The café gives Tory a new opportunity to get creative with his ingredients. For example, they can buy whole hogs from Willow Creek farm in Loganville, Wisconsin, and use all the parts by making bratwurst or other preserved meats for sale in the café. The best of both worlds, fine dining and casual eating, merge in an upstairs-downstairs format that increases access to sustainable foods to the Madison community and all of its hundreds of thousands of visitors.

Telling the story is as much a part of the work as finding and serving the freshest ingredients possible. When you walk into L'Etoile, to the right on a well-lit wall is a beautiful map of Wisconsin with all of the purveyors meticulously labeled. While Traci admits that they frequently have to add new ones, this front-and-center visual mapping of their farms shows how proud they are of the community the restaurant fosters and supports throughout the state.

> Throughout the peak of the season, Traci estimates that they source 95 to 97 percent of their ingredients locally.

Farm names are also always featured on their menu, something that their guests are very enthusiastic about. Throughout the peak of the season, Traci estimates that they source 95 to 97 percent of their ingredients locally, with wintertime averages around 75 to 80 percent. Another thing that makes L'Etoile unique is that they also have a farmer who waits tables a few nights each week. Kristen Kordet from Blue Moon Community Farm has been working at L'Etoile since 2004. "It's a natural fit to have a farmer on the floor—no one can describe the food better than someone who grew it," says Traci. "I wish we could get more farmers to work in the front of the house, although the late night hours make that difficult." Traci really values this unique relationship and the others that come with the business of creating new levels of awareness on both sides of the plate.

Farm 255: Local, Seasonal, and Sustainable in the South

By Olivia Sargeant, partner, general manager, and farmer

Athens, Georgia, is a town of anomalies. Despite it being the liberal bastion of the Deep South, the confederate flag waves strong on street corners, SEC football and deer hunting are common topics of conversation, and word-of-mouth is still the most effective communication strategy. Raising a restaurant and a farm within this geographic, socio-economic, and historical context has been the riskiest, most creative, and most rewarding endeavor of my life.

In October 2004, I moved from the Bay Area to Athens, Georgia, on the promise of a whim: with no restaurant experience (culinary or managerial) and no secure funding. Five friends and I had decided to open a restaurant attached to a farm. Four years later we are Farm 255, a 140-seat restaurant, full bar, and live music venue in conjunction with our farm, Full Moon Farms, an eight-acre biodynamic farm and seventy-five-member CSA. Most of our ingredients and all of our meat grows on our land, a quick four-mile truck ride away from our kitchen. We supplement our own harvests with those of other local small-scale and sustainable farmers and ranchers and purchase whole animals using all of the various cuts of meat throughout our menu. Our menu changes as often as the weather.

We were twenty-somethings when it began. We were always agriculturalists, gastronomes, manifesto writers, abattoir fiends, risky eaters . . . and now we are successful entrepreneurs. My partners and I, along with our dedicated team of employees, sow seeds by day and sauté by night. Our goal is to reestablish a local and sustainable food system while serving supper. But given how far we are from Alice Waters' entourage of foodie-chef-activists, we must serve a hefty portion of carefully tuned information alongside our collard greens and mash. In a place with little consciousness of the local food movement, we had to build an army of cooks, waiters, and patrons who would share our vision. We originally hired folks that were well versed in our ideals, and soon found that passionate activists don't make great waiters. And so we learned to seek capable, driven people and to teach them our ethics. We created a unique training program, including mandatory monthly farm chores and the occasional chicken kill, that gives rise to cross-pollination: line cooks herd our cows; bartenders book our bands; waiters build our furniture.

For us here at the farm, eating is a celebration of food's origins, the paths it travels on the way to our tables, and the lessons learned through the journey.

Our food acts as the intermediary between producers and consumers, urging people to discover and celebrate the source of their supper. Until a century ago, almost everything that everyone ate everywhere on earth was organic, free-range, artisanal, and locally grown or locally produced. It wasn't special or high-end, it was just food. We hope for our restaurant to help achieve that norm again, and make everyday food genuinely "good food": locally sourced, seasonal, steeped in tradition and narrative, connecting people to each other, to their community, and to their right to eat and live well.

JESSE ZIFF COOL

AUTHOR, CHEF AND
RESTAURATEUR,
FLEA STREET CAFÉ

Flea Street Café serves
simple, nurturing food
from organic ingredients.

"The customer comes last" is Chef Jesse Cool's mantra. For over thirty-five years, Jesse has repeated this on her road to becoming a vocal leader of local, sustainable, and organic cuisine. Jesse fosters strong connections with farmers, and the staff at her restaurant, Flea Street Café, is encouraged to do the same. The result is delicious food prepared by people who are connected and concerned. Customers, finally, can't help but feel nourished on many levels.

"It's nothing new," she says matter-of-factly. "What we're trying to do is apply old-world values to modern-day diets."

As a leader of the farm-to-restaurant movement since the 1970s, Jesse's commitment has expanded beyond organic farms and is focused on actively supporting the next generation of farmers. She is also helping educate people about how they can get involved via her approachable seasonal recipes and cookbooks, such as *Simply Organic*. Inspired by the farms of Northern California, she's written seven cookbooks featuring recipes for everyone. Jesse acknowledges the challenges in encouraging people to think about what's growing locally and even about organics—both critical components in sustainability. "We are Americans," she says with a smile, "and we want things now. But food doesn't work this way. We, as chefs and consumers, must embrace what is around us, and at times what is not. This is where I get the inspiration for my food—those moments each year when a certain flavor is at its best."

Her commitment to clean, organic foods "really came out of uncertainty and fear. [When I started] I didn't know what pesticides and food coloring were. I was accustomed to knowing where my food came from, and the thought of having chemicals on my food and exposing my staff was enough to make me committed to organic foods in my restaurant. I was already preparing whole and natural foods for my kids and it spilled over into the restaurant. My connection to farmers came a little later."

SUPPORTING THE HEALTH AND VITALITY OF THE COMMUNITY

Through the love and teachings of her parents and family, Jesse has made food and community health synonymous.

In her Italian-Jewish household, her mother and grandmother would make everything from scratch, with family time revolving around food. In addition, her grandparents and parents always used food—like garlic and citrus—as the primary defense in fighting off colds and the flu. But her family's discernment for good food didn't come without repercussions. To realize at age thirteen that everyone didn't have garlic breath, for example, was a big surprise: "I had an Italian boyfriend who told me, 'You smell of garlic,'" she remembers.

Edna, her grandmother, was a "remarkable cook" and taught Jesse how to make various pastas, sauces and whatever meat her Uncle Jack brought home. (Jack owned the local slaughterhouse and would break down naturally raised meats.)

Jesse's father, "King Eddie," ran the local grocery and was famous in their small blue-collar town. Even during hard years—in fact, especially in hard years—he would always extend his generosity to those in the community that needed it.

Jesse's dad would extol the importance of "helping your neighbor," since in the small town people knew each other well and everyone relied on the strength of the community. Jesse translates her father's principles by supporting her community's farms and nourishing her neighbors with clean, healthy food. And her mother, June, provided all of the unconditional love and support Jesse could ever hope for.

All of this accumulated knowledge has served her well while supporting small and sustainable farms and food businesses. Controversially, Jesse is also an advocate for some of the more mainstream producers such as Earthbound Farm, Cal-Organic, Cascadian Farm, and numerous others. All of these farms started off on just a few acres and all of them have grown to be very big, growing on large acreages but also contracting with networks of farmers to grow their food. These "industrial organic farms" are often rejected by the sustainable food movement due to their size and volume. However, Jesse has a different view. She feels that these producers open up the possibility of purchasing organic and sustainable foods to more people. They also tend to have the distribution mechanisms necessary to get the produce to more places. Her acceptance of this nuance of size is largely due to growing up in a colder climate where seasonality was limited. She still remembers the struggle to find local and organic foods while opening her first restaurant and feels that large producers mitigate this hurdle for food businesses trying to offer organic foods. She points out the large environmental impact that mainstream organic has made, to the tune of hundreds of thousands of pounds of pesticides and herbicides *not* used every year.

> "Be a zealot 80 percent of the time by focusing on good clean [organic/ sustainable] foods; the other 20 percent of the time, live in the real world and choose your poisons well."

SIMPLE AND NURTURING FOOD

While the number of women in professional kitchens is starting to catch up with men, it can be a disheartening and even demoralizing experience. "The hardest thing for many years," says Jesse, "was that I was a better cook than some men and had a better sense of feeding people. I didn't use erections, towers, visuals, or foam guns and didn't have to use any tricks to make my dishes bigger or better. Cooking real food with a French core of simplicity did not make me play mind games to get people to love my food." Jesse finds some men are often more intent on impressing diners, intellectualize too much about the food, and don't bring the care and wholesomeness to what they do. "When those guys would come into my kitchen to work with their smoke and mirrors, I would fire them. My food is far more feminine and seeks to nurture people."

The soulfulness of food comes from the heart and home, from someone who wants to feed and nourish. Women bring the old and the new world to the table with a sophisticated elegance.

SUPPORTING THE NEW CROP OF FARMERS

Jesse's latest innovation as a business that supports local food and farmers is to connect and support young farmers. With farmers aging in this country—according to the last census the average age is up to fifty-seven—it is imperative that we encourage new farmers.[3] The main way to do this is to provide economic means and incentives—the biggest element missing in today's farm economy.

"At Eco Farm [an annual sustainable agriculture conference], I met a UC Santa Cruz graduate whose father is a grain farmer in Half Moon Bay," says Jesse. "We're going to buy everything they grow. I've learned how to set up my kitchen [with this flexibility] and it's a symbiotic relationship that we can work with. There are ways that we can work with whatever a farm has. If it's big and ugly we'll make soup. Our commitment is to that farm and not a particular menu item." She's currently partnering with three emerging farms in the San Mateo area.

Jesse's civic involvement extends past the doors of her restaurants and catering company. She has been on the board of directors of the Ecological Farming Association (EFA) for over twenty years and has served on numerous advisory committees including Slow Food, Chef's Collaborative, and Monterey Bay Aquarium's Sustainable Fish. Additionally, she now works with Stanford University to revamp their hospital food service starting with the most basic of comfort foods—soup. While she absolutely prioritizes organic and sustainable foods, she also lives by the following 80/20 rule, a rule she highlights in her cookbook, *Simply Organic:* "Be a zealot 80 percent of the time by focusing on good clean [organic/sustainable] foods; the other 20 percent of the time, live in the real world and choose your poisons well."

LOIS ELLEN FRANK

AUTHOR AND NATIVE FOODS HISTORIAN

CHEF AT RED MESA CUISINE

Red Mesa is a catering company Lois started with chef Walter Whitewater of the Navajo Nation. The company serves ancient Native American foods with a modern twist.

CULINARY ANTHROPOLOGIST

Lois is completing her PhD on the discourse and practice of Native American Cuisine, Native and non-Native chefs and cooks in contemporary kitchens.

Lois Ellen Frank has a penchant for flavor, for capturing the visual that goes along with it, and most of all, for documenting the foodways of Native American tribes across North and South America. Born and raised on Long Island, Lois's heritage is Kiowa on her mother's side and Sephardic on her father's side. Through her travels, photography, and eventual entry into academia, Lois has successfully created the new field of study called "Culinary Anthropology," focusing on ethnographic contemporary chefs and the foods they prepare. This has led her on a mission to preserve Native foods of North, Central, and South America with an emphasis on the Southwest Indian Nations (also the name of her book), while working to raise the visibility of Native American food's contributions to modern American cuisine. She has worked on more than eighteen cookbooks and twenty culinary posters that document this diversity and abundance.

While earning her bachelor of arts in photography, Lois discovered her calling would be in food. She spent some time working in advertising as a food photographer but "missed working with chefs and the foods that they prepared." Eventually she formed a partnership with her friend Mark Miller, a renowned chef who had worked at Chez Panisse with Alice Waters. Lois and Mark traveled to Mexico and South America, researching chilies and producing what became known as "The Great Chile Posters." Many posters later, Lois had fallen in love with her new lens as "researcher" and the fact that it integrated her three main passions: knowledge of food, an eye for capturing the beauty of food, and her passion for Native foods and the contributions these foods have given to the world. Pursuing a masters degree at the University of New Mexico's Anthropology department, Lois chose to focus her thesis on the importance of

"My goal in life is to walk into a supermarket and find the 'Native foods' aisle."

corn for indigenous populations on the American continent. Corn is sacred to Native peoples of the Americas due to its spiritual uses as well as its use for sustenance. "There is no one universal way of looking at corn, but in different tribal groups, corn is maiden, corn is mother, corn is healer, corn is medicine." Lois explains that "corn represents the four colors of man on this Earth; they form the medicine wheel and the circle of life. Corn is to the Americas what wheat is to Europe and rice is to Asia. It is the dominant grain that has sustained huge populations for thousands of years as a major cultivar."

LEARNING FROM NATIVE FOODWAYS

Over the centuries, humans have been courted by food's delicious flavors, nutritional content, and other valuable properties. This ensured the plants and animals that they would be prolific through the thinning, harvesting, and travel provided by the human species. Some of these co-evolved foods include the meats of bison, sheep, deer, wild turkey, abalone, and clam; vegetables and wild greens like corn, celery, carrots, nettles, and onions; fruits such as blueberries, lingonberry, and cactus; grains of wild rice; and acorn and piñon nuts. There is no need for daily vitamins or supplements in the Native American diet—these whole foods are nutrient dense. For example, the oily piñon nut that sustained tribal members in the absence of meat has almost all of the essential amino acids known to be necessary to human life. Lois explains that these "wild harvested foods" represent "acceptance gardening. We accept what nature provides and we adjunct it. The environment responds to our activity. An example of this is the prickly pear. Once a fruit is plucked from its body, the plant, knowing that it has been harvested, can put out twice as many fruits the following year."

In an interview at Bioneers, Lois emphasized the importance of taking only what is needed. "You must only harvest enough. You never go in and desecrate or harvest more than the patch can sustain. One of the faults that we've seen in the past, especially with American ginseng or Osha root, a root used for treating cold and flu symptoms of the upper respiratory tract, is that people say, 'Oh, this good for you and we can harvest this,' and they take it all."

Lois points out, "When I do education, I talk about local foods, most of which are organic—the term 'organic' was never a part of Native American ideology because Native peoples never sprayed anything anyway—so when I talk about local I use the terms 'Natively sourced,' foods sourced from a Native food producer, and 'sustainably sourced,' foods produced anywhere with sustainable methods. These are the circles I work within when I buy foods."

Lois ranks her food buying preferences as the following:

- Local and seasonal foods—coming from as close to home as possible
- Native foods—traditionally grown and raised plants and animals that represent a relationship with nature and have been produced by a Native American enterprise
- Organic—certified or not, practitioners that grow without pesticides and herbicides
- Fairly traded—foods from other countries that are produced in a sustainable way that benefits the land and communities they are grown in, and that have been produced by farmers and food producers who have been paid fair wages

PROMOTING NATIVE FOODS THROUGH MODERN CUISINE

Lois exemplifies a new thinking that goes beyond local. Since Native foods aren't on the radars of most of the country's chefs, yet, she's setting a new level of priority through her sourcing and education that happens through her catering company. Lois started Red Mesa Cuisine with another Native chef, Walter Whitewater, who is from the Diné (Navajo) Nation. At an event in August 2008 (Slow Food Nation), Red

Mesa was serving a stew with bison meat raised by Picuris Pueblo, a member of the Intertribal Bison cooperative. Also on the menu were New Mexico Pueblo blue corn posole and white corn posole soup. With her vast knowledge, Lois and Bernadette Zambrano of the Cultural Conservancy curated the Native Foods portion of the Taste Pavilion at the event, just one of the ways she helps educate through food.

During their day-to-day catering, Lois and Walter promote the use of Native foods that are locally sourced and organic, emphasizing the exceptional quality and flavor these foods have in addition to their cultural significance. In planning for a recent catering event, she describes how a client went through a whole "rigmarole" because of the price of the locally raised Navajo Churro lamb that Lois planned to use. "I said, 'Look, if you really want me to source lamb that is not local, I can get it for you, but you've really lost the essence of hiring me to do this." Lois and the client finally agreed to remove one of the take-home goodies from the menu in order to purchase the locally raised lamb. It was the right choice, as her guests raved about how good the food was—especially the lamb. Says Lois, "It is always worth it in the end to serve locally raised organic products that taste superior to any other."

In her love of flavor and seasonality that she brings to her clients at Red Mesa, she brings them something else too. She coaches her staff to be considerate of how they handle food and teaches that they need to leave all of their problems at the door of her kitchen. She wants her staff to be of "pure mind, body, spirit, and essence so that we conscientiously feed people with a concern—with love like your grandmother would, and with the essence of sustainability." She says, "Imagine if all the people that handle our food—from the time that it was a seed in the ground to the moment it is in the chef's hands—said 'Look how magnificent this food is' before sending it on. If we all treated growing, cooking, and eating food with this 'non-tangible essence,' with genuine concern and care for nurturing and feeding each other, it could change the nutritional component of what we eat and how we approach life."

Despite Lois's optimism of how much potential there is for Native foods to receive their just desserts, she is painfully aware of how quickly we lose the knowledge and the ways of our food. She believes that Native foods contain stories that will disappear if they are not continually handed down from generation to generation. "We need to go back, all of us, and ask our elders the story of who we are and the foods that represent us and why we do what we do in our own family lineages. We need to perpetuate these stories and revitalize them and celebrate diversity. When we celebrate diversity it doesn't fracture us, it joins us."

Lois's dream to be able to go into a store and say, "Excuse me, where is the Native Foods aisle?" and hear the clerk reply, "Aisle three." She envisions a day when that aisle will have all of the food from the various cultures that have contributed to Native American cuisine, from pre-contact (before settlers), to first contact and beyond. These foods contain hidden treasures of health and environmental wisdom that are there for us to cultivate and to learn from. "Someday," says Lois excitedly, "we'll walk in and there *will* be a Native food aisle and we'll find Tonka bars made from bison meat and ground cranberries like the ancestors used to eat, and wild rice from the Ojibwe Nation, and bison meat from the plains, and blue corn posole grown the traditional way by the Pueblo ancestors, and Northwest Coast salmon, and all the foods that make up Native American cuisine."

Through her work and practice of experiencing various food cultures and traditions, Lois has found a commonality. "Food is universal. We don't need to speak the same language to sit at the same table and eat together. The secret is to celebrate and keep alive the pockets of cultural traditions, of diversity, so beautiful like the seeds. There is richness in that."

RECIPES FOR ACTION

*S*easonal menu planning, shopping, and eating locally require a little bit of extra effort. But after you get into the routine of buying local, Native, and heirloom foods, it will become second nature. Here are some suggestions on how to do it. (Make sure to check out the Resources section too.)

EATER

As an eater, your task is to enjoy, encourage and eat delicious local, Native, organic, fairly traded and heirloom foods. Sound easy enough? Here are some ways to advocate through your plate:

- Ask for local foods wherever you eat and shop.
- Buy Native and heirloom varieties of foods as often as possible.
- Invite friends over for a special meal highlighting heirloom foods, or throw a potluck with a Native or heirloom theme.
- Join Slow Food and support their "Ark of Taste" project.
- Volunteer or support organizations working to preserve our food diversity. (See Resources for list.)

FARMER

Growing diversity on your farm will mean that varieties will be around for future generations. Additionally, you can:

- Grow heirloom and Native foods on your farm.
- Partner with organizations to do seed trials on your property, such as Seeds of Change or Seed Savers Exchange. (See Resources section).
- Work with Slow Food to promote and publicize your efforts.
- Host an event on your farm to educate the public about what you grow/raise.

FOOD BUSINESS

Whenever you can, buy local, sustainable, native and organic. To support a more sustainable and diversified food system, you can:

- Give your customers the choice by educating them about your offerings. They'll let you know that sourcing with the aforementioned factors in mind will be supported.

- Create a special menu based on Native foods.
- Partner with Slow Food to host an event.
- Donate to one of the organizations in the Resources section, or host an event.

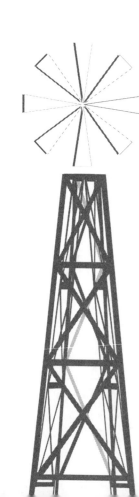

CHAPTER 4

NETWORKS FOR SUSTAINABLE FOOD

F ood is a great instigator for advocacy, and the women of this chapter exemplify this through their passion in changing how we eat and farm.

Demonstrated by the thousands of people brought together around the country by the networks they have created, these women are working to raise the visibility of, and create solutions for, a more sustainable food system.

Women-led agricultural groups, or networks, date back to the early 1900s but at the time were primarily outcroppings of industry associations. The Pork Association, for example, funded the "Porkettes," and the "Dairy Maids" were supported by the National Dairy Association. It's only been in the past thirty-five years that women have shifted toward leading nonprofit organizations and networks, determined to counter the impacts of our industrial food system gone awry.

Advocating for family farmers, local food, farm worker rights, and cultural and biological diversity, the women in this chapter work with a multitude of partners, colleagues, and stakeholders to make their vision a reality. From an impassioned Midwestern farmer who co-founded the Women, Food and Agriculture Network, a leader of the Buy Fresh Buy Local movement that has swept the nation, an activist for Latina farm workers and their families, and an advocate of reviving Native American philosophy of growing food in harmony with the earth, each of the women is succeeding in her efforts to create a truly sustainable food system for the United States that respects the people and the environment.

What's truly unique about these women is that they have been able to ignite broad community support, both in their state and oftentimes nationally, for their cause.

DENISE O'BRIEN

The peaceful agrarian scene on Denise O'Brien's farm—white fence, barn, and tractor in the yard; humans, plants, and animals evident on the landscape—belies the lively activist life Denise leads as a sustainable farmer and promoter of women's leadership roles in agriculture. One of the founders of the Women, Food and Agriculture Network (WFAN), an organization that works to empower women as leaders in the sustainable agriculture industry, Denise, along with her farmer husband, Larry, provides diversified organic foods for her community. While many other Iowa farms specialize in two crops—corn and soybeans—Rolling Acres Farm provides both meat birds for the holidays, and strawberries and mixed vegetables for the farm's twenty devoted CSA (Community Supported Agriculture) customers during the summer months.

ROLLING ACRES FARM AND ACTIVISM

Growing up on a farm in Atlantic, Iowa, with three sisters and four brothers, Denise would eventually return to farming as a livelihood in her mid-twenties. But first she had to go searching for her path elsewhere. The Vietnam War, which was raging while Denise was in high school and college, ultimately influenced the activist path she would pursue. After living in the San Francisco Bay Area during the late 1960s and early '70s—during the heart of the hippie antiwar movement—Denise ended up back in her hometown of Atlantic to take care of her family and be closer to home after farming for a stint in Vermont. She had planned to return to the East Coast after awhile, but instead met her future husband, Larry Harris, after he introduced himself as someone who wanted to farm organically. The two immediately hit it off. The happy young couple were married the next spring in the community that they both grew up in and immediately started Rolling Acres Farm.

In the late 1970s, organic farming did not command much respect in Atlantic. Yet, even though Denise and Larry's agricultural practices were radically different from those of their neighbors, the fact that they were both born in Atlantic eased much of their neighbors' unrest. They continued farming their own way until the 1980s Farm Crisis—a dismal time when one in four farms in the Midwest foreclosed—when they were called into action.

As various calamities occurred on Denise and Larry's farm and in their community, the two launched themselves into advocacy, hosting the first Iowa Farm Unity Coalition meeting in 1982. Around that time, Denise and Larry made the decision that Larry would stay home, raise the kids, and tend to the farm while she traveled around representing family farmers.

Despite her husband being a progressive feminist, Denise often encountered less-than-supportive male comrades while she attended, organized, and facilitated farmer meetings.

"It's important for women to be involved in decision-making, from a family level to the highest level of government. It isn't always easy. Many times people are threatened by a woman who speaks her mind," says Denise. This reality can make for a lonely and isolating experience, but Denise stayed strong. At one point in the creation of an organization she was helping organize, Denise offered to take a lead and her male counterpart told her she wasn't ready for a leadership role. "There were setbacks all along and it culminated in the 1980s when I was tired of working with men that were reluctant to let women step up to the plate," she remembers.

"It's important for women to be involved in decision-making from a family level to the highest levels of government."

Undeterred and looking to make more of an impact, Denise eventually refocused her interest to advocating on behalf of women farmers. One of Denise's first activities with women agricultural producers was the Homestead Pride Poultry Co-op in 1990, when she and other women poultry producers pooled their chickens to sell to institutions, retailers, and restaurants. By pooling their birds for higher volumes and collaboratively branding their product, they were able to access more markets than they could have as individual farms. This project was a successful venture between women and one that fueled Denise to continue working to support women farmers.

THE WOMEN, FOOD AND AGRICULTURE NETWORK

With continued support from her family, Denise was elected and served as president of the National Family Farm Coalition (NFFC) from 1993 to 1995. (The NFFC is a national network that advocates on behalf of family farmers and rural communities.) During this time she also started thinking more strategically about women farmer networks and what her next steps would be in advocating for equal rights. Along

The Food Conspiracy

In the 1970s Denise was involved with a "food conspiracy" that formed in the Bay Area. ("Leave it to California to call it a conspiracy," says Denise.) Influenced by the first Earth Day in 1972, and the release of Rachel Carson's book Silent Spring, The Food Conspiracy was born out of an interest by people to have better quality food that was sustainable. People were becoming more aware of various pollutants used in our food systems—the pesticides, herbicides, and other petrochemicals—and pioneered ways of avoiding them through food conspiracies.

Resembling a modern day member-owned food co-op, the Conspiracy required members to provide ten minutes of work for each item they ordered. Organizing the food pantry, cleaning the aisles, and other tasks like shopping for food would account for a time contribution. Much like the Community Supported Agriculture (CSA) with a number of women, Denise was able to successfully form the Women, Food and Agriculture Network (WFAN) in 1997—an organization that meshed with her vision for a sustainable food and farming system that empowered women as leaders.

WFAN, one of the earliest women-led sustainable food networks in the country, started by providing resources to the growing number of women entering more "formalized" leadership roles on their farms. Surveying women farmers about their needs, WFAN found that women farmers were seeking networking opportunities with other women producers to talk about good farming practices, to troubleshoot machinery problems, and to share information about government and nonprofit resources. WFAN has worked ever since to help end women's isolation in farming and agriculture and to recognize the role women play, in both the front of the house (public side) and the back of the house (behind the scenes), in making our food and farming more environmentally and economically viable.

> The Women, Food and Agriculture Network was created to help end women's isolation in farming and agriculture.

model, members often learned to cook with foods that they'd never heard of—Asian greens, chards, kales and rutabagas—and other things that were in season and available at the wholesale produce markets (the equivalent of our farmers markets today).

As an example of one of the early food networks, the Conspiracy on the West Coast and co-ops of the East represented a unified vision for people wanting to support a localized and more humane food system. Today, Food

Conspiracies are definitely back in fashion, and the great news is that you can even start your own (see Recipes for Action, page 160).

Not only does Denise farm and work on sustainable agriculture issues, but she also finds time to mentor innumerable women every year, sharing her skills, passion, and thirty-plus years of connections to the "rising stars," as she calls them. As a delegate representing U.S. women farmers, Denise has traveled to Belgium, China, Costa Rica, Cuba, France, Mexico, the Netherlands, Spain, the former Soviet Union, and to Rome in 2004 to participate in the United Nations Food and Agriculture Organization's Committee on Agriculture. In 2006, she settled into her home state to run for Secretary of Agriculture, sticking close to her farm roots for a little while. Although she didn't win, the experience gave her a stronger commitment to developing policy that will help build a nation of small farmers.

Last summer, Denise decided to give one hundred heirloom Bourbon Red chickens a go along with her standard white turkeys. The dark red–plumed birds are making a comeback despite their decline after being widely commercialized in the 1950s.[1] Denise watched as the beautiful new additions to her brood ran around her yard, grubbing and getting fat, and she thought about her next steps in the food and farming world.

"It's been a very privileged life with all that I've accomplished," she says, "and there's still so much more to do! When winter settles in and I'm at home, I get that itchy feeling that I've got to do something." And "do something" she does.

Why a Network for Women in Sustainable Agriculture?

Leigh Adcock, *Executive Director, Women, Food and Agriculture Network (WFAN)*

One of the most surprising things I encountered after becoming executive director of WFAN was that even our organizational allies in sustainable agriculture don't always understand why women need their own network within the movement. Why couldn't we find what we needed as members of their groups? Were we saying that men couldn't be part of the sustainable food movement? Were we (my favorite question) all lesbians?

The reality is that women in every profession still need our own networks because we remain woefully under-represented in decision-making positions. In the sustainable agriculture movement and within the institutions that shape the policy that in turn shapes our food system, we do not occupy many positions of power. Regardless, women continue to drive much of the positive change by purchasing healthy local food for our families and by becoming food producers.

WFAN is a community of women involved in sustainable agriculture. We are farmers, landowners, researchers, students, advocates, and mothers concerned about our families' health. We come from all over the United States and several other countries, and do the majority of our work in the Midwest.

Women own or co-own 47 percent of the farmland in Iowa,[2] and the number of women farmland owners is rising nationally.[3] WFAN exists so that women can give each other the information, connections, and encouragement needed to be effective practitioners and supporters of sustainable agriculture and healthy localized food systems.

In some regions of developing African nations and much of Asia, women produce up to 90 percent of the food supply and provide 70 percent of the agriculture labor but own less than 2 percent of the land.[4] With the increased role of mechanization and industrialization in American agriculture since World War II, women have become less and less responsible for food production in our country. As more and more Americans begin to realize the harm that industrialized food production causes our health, economy, and social structures, women are beginning to reclaim their places as producers. The 2007 U.S. Census of Agriculture showed that women operators are increasing in number nationwide, even as the number of overall farmers decreases. They are particularly strongly represented in the market-farm segment—in other words, growing food and other farm products for direct and Internet sales.

One of WFAN's most successful projects arose out of our recognition that women communicate their values about land and agriculture differently from the way men do:

- Women tend to speak of their land as a community resource rather than a commodity.
- They are highly concerned about conservation and land stewardship.
- They prefer to learn new information from other women who are practicing conservation and are willing to share their stories.
- They prefer informal dialogue to classroom-style presentations, and they would rather have a speaker come to meet with them as a group than go alone to the Farm Service Agency or Natural Resources Conservation Service offices to try to retrieve the information they want.

As a result of these findings, WFAN created a project in Iowa called "Women Caring for the Land," which brings women landowners (owner-operators, co-owners, and inheritors) together in "learning circles" within their own communities to share information on conservation and land stewardship. These landowners need accurate information on what conservation techniques and programs are available, advice on the way conservation can be worked into a lease agreement with their tenant or share-cropper, and techniques or personal help with negotiating the leases with their tenants.

Another crucial element of food system reform is cultivating beginning farmers. Women all over the country are exploring and beginning rural businesses including market farms, specialty shops, and bed-and-breakfast enterprises. Currently we are building a database of women who own farmland and women who want to farm so that we can help them find each other and transition as much farmland as possible to sustainable methods.

As concerns for food safety and security, health, and economic and social justice continue pressuring America to transform its food system we predict that women will play an ever more important role in this transformation. For decades, women have helped to drive the sustainable agriculture movement, and now that the movement is becoming more mainstream, we must continue to guide and shape it at all levels of society, from the farm to the halls of Congress. WFAN exists to facilitate this effort, "linking and empowering women to build food systems and communities that are healthy, just, sustainable, and that promote environmental integrity."

JESSICA GREENBLATT SEELEY

MANAGER,
FOODROUTES
NETWORK

FoodRoutes is a national organization that promotes family farmers and local foods.

FARMER, MILKY WAY FARMS

Milky Way Farms is an organic dairy farm in Troy, Pennsylvania.

As evidenced through her dedication as manager of the FoodRoutes Network, Jessica "Jess" Greenblatt Seeley possesses an unwavering love for food and community.

Growing up in the suburbs of New Jersey, Jess didn't become a farm girl and food advocate until studying in State College, Pennsylvania. Between her hours spent earning her degree in geography and minor in agronomy, Jess earned her green thumb on the weekends working for a woman that owned a small farm on the outskirts of town. Falling in love with the lifestyle inevitably brought Jess to Milky Way Farms, where she lives with her husband, Shon, in rural Pennsylvania.

It's here that she has successfully blended farm life with food activism as she helps with the farm and manages FoodRoutes, a national organization that promotes family farmers and local foods, from the farm-based home office.

THE BEAUTY OF SMALL FARMS

While Jess's undergraduate studies consisted of numerous courses focused on industrial-size agriculture, outside of school she was drawn to the scale of production at Full Circle Farm—small, diversified, and growing for the direct markets of State College, composed of university students and employees, and numerous restaurants. It was in one of her agronomy classes that she met he future husband, Shon— "the only guy not wearing a Monsanto or Cargill hat," Jess remembers. After graduating, she decided to delve deeper into farming and went to work for the inspiring community supported agriculture (CSA) innovator Elizabeth Henderson (see page 21). There Jess learned that a farm can run like clockwork. The systems, the seasons, and the operations of the farm were the smoothest she had ever seen.

Shon, on the other hand, grew up on the four-hundred-acre farm that he, his parents, and his grandparents have kept in the family since the 1920s, a dairy farm that transitioned to organic before organic was even a certification.

Shon's dad, Kim, farmed the family land conventionally utilizing an arsenal of chemicals (byproducts of World War II and the petroleum industry) that he had learned at Penn State until he realized how unsafe it was for his family. "When Shon was two years old," recounts Jess, "Kim found him climbing on a corn planter barrel of treatment chemicals. He stopped using chemicals on the farm that day, deciding that he wanted everything on the farm to be safe, whether someone was two or eighty years old." Kim's decision to transition the farm to organic in the 1970s has left 220 acres of the farm as open wilderness with scenic woodlands that harbor birds, bats, deer, bobcats, possum, and other critters that are ultimately part of a balanced ecosystem.

As petroleum-based inputs of fertilizers and chemicals become expensive for farmers, the "old ways" will again be revisited—alternating crops; rotating animals (cows, chickens, etc.) around to various fields for grazing and fertilizing with their manure; diversifying plantings to attract beneficial insects and reduce crop loss; growing nitrogen-fixing crops to amend the soil; and letting the land sit idle for a few years to allow it to rejuvenate. While farming to maintain, and even increase, the fertility of the land may take more time, proponents of sustainable farming believe that the importance of keeping in balance with nature outweighs perceived barriers. Even though the traditional way of farming makes the most ecological and economic sense by reducing synthetic, off-farm inputs such as fertilizers and pesticides, we have long a way to go before our chemical-addicted lands will be converted to the natural working spaces they were in pre-industrial-agriculture years—especially as the government still allocates the majority of our taxpayer subsidies to some of the most environmentally destructive crops (corn, wheat, soy, and cotton).

Milky Way Farms, conversely, has become a success story by virtue of its early adoption of organic farming practices, maintaining the dairy through economically depressed times throughout its history.

The farm's diner, an example of business diversification and a relic from the farm's early days, has also helped keep the farm strong today. Started by Shon's grandparents in 1960, "The Milky Way Diner literally started selling meals because the whole town knew that Marie Seeley, Shon's grandmother, could bake a mean pie," says Jess. After raising four farm kids, it's no surprise that she would be accustomed to feeding a crowd. Today she bakes upwards of eight pies every day except Sunday, when the diner is closed. According to Jess, "Marie refuses the use of a cookbook, measuring spoon, or other formal culinary tools," making them from memory. Of her eight varieties, she's most renowned for her huckleberry pie, using berries that foragers gather in the nearby Armenia Mountains each fall. Marie freezes bucket-loads of these wild delights to ensure a year-round stock. While the prices of the diner's food have changed over the years, the place retains its charm and old-fashioned décor, such as the clock Shon's grandfather installed when the diner opened. Today, in addition to a hearty meal and great pie, locals stop in to pick up milk, cheese, and other dairy products made right there on the farm.

FINDING HER FOODROUTES

After her experience of farming at Peacework Organic Farm, Jess's desire for advocacy eventually led her to a position working as an organic certifier with Pennsylvania Certified Organic (PCO), the state's independent organic certifying agency. The majority of her work consisted of certifying dairy cows of Amish farmers, who still farm the natural way after all these years. Pennsylvania is the third-largest dairy state after California and Wisconsin, with an average organic dairy herd of forty-five cows compared to the larger dairy-producing states such as California, whose medium-sized organic dairy farms hover around 1,300.[5]

It was while working with Pennsylvania Organic that Jess was introduced to a newer initiative in food and farm advocacy: FoodRoutes.

"Back in 2000 FoodRoutes brought together leaders in the sustainable food movement to figure out what the missing pieces were," says Jess. "The resounding answer was that farmers needed help marketing their products." While marketing tends to fall to the bottom of the list for farmers who are preoccupied with growing food, tracking the weather, maintaining farm equipment, and juggling various small business operations, it is arguably one of the most important parts of any small business. FoodRoutes was responsible for leading the charge of helping farms and consumers create more vibrant local food economies and today bolsters partners in over thirty-five states.

Jess came on in 2007 to help grow the organization's national Buy Fresh Buy Local campaign, which was created in 2002 to address the lack of information in stores about where food is coming from. FoodRoutes had commissioned a consumer study that found that 75 percent of people would choose locally grown foods if they had origin information available when selecting food—even if it were more expensive. This study became the premise for FoodRoutes to launch Buy Fresh Buy Local in 2002 in four states—California, Iowa, Louisiana and Pennsylvania. Partnering with a graphic design team called Design for Social Impact, FoodRoutes resuscitated the iconic fruit-and-vegetable-crate label of yesteryear to appeal to people's taste buds and memory of wholesome, family-farmed foods. The label is adapted to each growing region to represent the foods that are local to an area. Each region (sometimes as many as five or six per state) has its own "toolkit" complete with banner-sized logos, bumper sticker graphics, and other elements to get the word out about local foods.

With increasing demand for farm-identified products, information on origin, local flavor, and a real, honest connection to family farmers, FoodRoutes has seen tremendous growth in their network since the implementation of the Buy Fresh Buy Local campaign. Its expansion from four to over seventy-three chapters across thirty-five states proves the campaign's timeliness and resonance with communities. Such activities undoubtedly

FoodRoutes helps farmers with marketing their products, arguably one of the most important parts of any small business.

led the USDA to announce their "Know your farmer, know your food" program in late 2009. The popularity of such campaigns and marketing has undoubtedly pushed industrial producers and their retail markets to vie for the same audiences as those that shop at the growing number of farmers markets and natural and organic food stores.

"It's been amazing—networks are really thriving," says Jess. "There's wonderful diversity—urban, rural, low-income, and others that are sharing their lessons learned through our conference calls and annual meetings. We continue to grow at about fifteen chapters per year."

THE RURAL LIFE

On the farm, Jess can be found in the bottling plant helping out her

Value Added Foods

V alue added" refers to anything that is transformed from its raw ingredients into something else—cheeses, jams and jellies, canned tomatoes, yogurt, dried fruit, sausages, cereal, bread. This process of product transformation has come under such scrutiny and regulation of late that it has become a sore spot for many farmers who want to transform their foods into something with more shelf life. Contrary to popular and mandated Public Health Department codes, foods do not need to be prepared in a "certified" kitchen to be safe. A "certified kitchen" requires washing stations, ramps, bathrooms, and stainless-steel everything, and, not surprisingly, it costs a small fortune.

Such expensive certification processes keep farmers from selling their jams to their community and parents from selling baked goods for school fundraisers.

While this is, and should be, the case for products sold in pallets, unfortunately the small farmer is viewed the same way as agribusiness in the eyes of our regulating agencies. This means that the small-scale production of fresh cheese, milk, preserves and pies— the kinds of foods people used to make in their homes and provide for their communities—has become a nearly criminal activity. More great information about these foods and this challenge to creating local food systems can be found in The Revolution Will Not Be Microwaved by Sandor Katz (see Bibliography).

husband and in-laws sometimes twice a week, in between working at her local food advocacy job. "I call myself the pinch hitter, coming in to lend a hand whenever it's needed—especially on bottling or cheese-making days. Bottling milk is quite the process—especially with older equipment. I can always tell if my husband needs a hand by the look on his face," she laughs. The Seeleys' milk-bottling production happens in an area at the back of the store that is only big enough to fit three people. Jess describes the milk as "the most beautiful milk ever. It has a nice, rich yellow color from the grass." In addition to selling goods to locals, the farm also sells to the local college and nearby schools. They've changed their production schedule to meet the demand of this market, which is heavy in fall and spring but slow in summer—just the opposite of most dairy farms. This innovation has brought them additional success in marketing their dairy, along with their recent foray into cheese making.

Cheese has been on the radar of the farm for years. Led by a local woman cheese maker and dear family friend, Milky Way Farms is in the process of trying out various cheddar and jack cheeses from their organic heifers. "There's a huge learning curve. Making cheese is a 7:00 a.m. to 9:00 p.m. kind of ordeal—you can't just stop in the middle of it and go eat dinner. Everything is really precise—temperature, stirring, cooling, and cutting," says Jess. Milky Way currently makes about six varieties of cheddar and jack, which they sell at the farm store, to a local coffee shop, and to some restaurants. "We're hesitant to do a large cheese caveat of the farm. We live in a rural area and our community is our market. We don't think we would be able to sell a product that would require our neighbors to pay a higher price than they're used to." So for now, they're keeping their cheese line on the smaller end to meet the demand of the markets available to them.

"Out here, Bradford County's per capita income is about $20,000 per year. There's not a lot of wiggle room for more expensive food items," she says. "Our town has two restaurants: one a pizza place and the other Chinese. They don't really provide a substantial market for us." Local food may provide a point of pride for their community, but they've found that the finances are not typically there to support the economics of it. So for Milky Way Farm, the majority of their sales remain outside of their community to the aforementioned universities, schools and a few local businesses.

While not everyone is rushing back to the land (yet) to try her hand at farming, each of us needs to eat everyday and ideally, that food will be from as close to home as possible. "Food is the universal common denominator," says Jess, "especially considering that the restaurant industry, food service sector, and other businesses are dependent on raw food products to create foods at their processing facilities."

"We need more farmers, and we need more people supporting farming; if a suburban Asian Jewish girl can farm, so can anyone."

Despite the challenges of managing a national network of non-profits while living on a farm, Jess is convinced that the timely message of eating and supporting local foods is making a big impact. Her draw into farming came out of various experiences, ones that she hopes other women will feel confident in being able to attain as well. "I hope there are other girls out there who learn about their inner farmer and get to know farms the way I have," she says. "We need more farmers, and we need more people supporting farming; if a suburban Asian Jewish girl can farm, so can anyone. Regardless of where this takes me, the local food movement is in my life whether or not I'm working in it or helping Shon with the dairy."

MILY TREVIÑO-SAUCEDA

FOUNDER,
ORGANIZACIÓN
DE LÍDERES
CAMPESINAS

The organization is a
support network for
women farm workers
in California.

Mily Treviño-Sauceda's story, one of advocacy for social justice for women farm workers, started in the fields. Her childhood experiences of hard work and labor led her to start the first women's farm worker organization in the country—Líderes Campesinas (Women Farmworker Leaders). Mily started the organization with key supporters in the 1990s to provide a critical support network for women farm workers in California. By helping *campesinas* access healthcare information, providing networking opportunities, and advocating for social justice and human rights within the largest food economy of the United States, they are able to effect change that extends beyond the borders of the state.

When we think about our food and our farmers, we often think about land, families, tractors, iconic red barns. But the behind the scenes work—the seeding, planting, pruning, pinching, and harvesting of plants and animals—is still largely invisible. Our food still requires a surprising amount of hand labor. Despite our country's labor laws, our food comes from the fields from migrant workers laboring for less than minimum wage. With little legal recourse and health care options despite the dangers of the profession, these are some of the most exploited workers in the United States.

Upwards of 75 percent of our farm workers come from Mexico, through special contracts or illegally, to work in the various crops and harvests.[6] These jobs are in high enough demand to make the treacherous Mexico border crossings with *coyotes* worth the risk.

MIGRANT TRAIL

Mily experienced the life of a farm worker firsthand while growing up. She and two of her brothers were born in Bellingham, Washington, while the rest of her seven siblings were born and stayed in Mexico in her family's hometown of Linares.

Their work as a family started in Blackfoot, Idaho, in the 1960s, where the five of them worked in the fields moving irrigation lines. "We were paid by the number of watering lines we moved," says Mily, and not by the hour. "I believe my parents' social security numbers were the only ones used. We were too small to report any earnings . . . my parents were not paid much for our work either."

Disconnecting, lifting, and setting pipes is grueling work—especially for a child of eight years. Mily remembers the painful weight of the pipes, some of which had twenty-odd pieces and weighed fifty pounds each. "They were so heavy," she says. "I used to pick them up by myself." Hernias and severe back pain still afflict her two brothers from the toll of this work on their young bodies. Working with her parents and brothers in the fields for two to three hours before school, and up to an additional five hours afterwards, made them sleepy and seemingly disinterested while in their classes. "By mid-afternoon we would be falling asleep," she says. "And the teachers did not pay attention to us as it was hard for them to communicate in Spanish." It didn't help that while migrating to various fields the children frequently switched schools while living out of their car—making their lives even more tumultuous during those critical years of growth and development.

Mily's academic performance was starkly contrasted when the family would return to Linares for the holidays and she would attend classes in her native tongue. In Linares, Mily was a straight-A student.

It was during these annual pilgrimages in winter that she would re-experience home. The four- to five-day drive was always instigated by her mom, who, longing for family and tradition, always petitioned to make the drive. While they were in Mexico, they "did not live very poor, but in the U.S. we lived very poor while we were migrating," she says. In Mexico, they had family and friends that provided for their needs, a house to stay in and school with a language they understood. Despite this, it was always the opportunity to work and make more money that drove the family back to the U.S. each time. In Mexico, there weren't any jobs—a scenario that is still true today, in large part due to U.S. foreign policy that has displaced farmers from their fields in Mexico.[7]

Migrant farm workers and their children continue to experience the same degenerate working conditions that Mily and her family dealt with. As opposed to permanent, year-round workers on farms, migrant workers are vulnerable to mistreatment as they are less likely to have information of their rights available to them in new cities. Disempowered by the newness of a place and language, they are often exploited by farms and labor contractors. Despite the need for agricultural workers in the U.S., without legal migrant status, they fear repercussions for seeking out even the most basic of human rights, including access to bathroom facilities, translation assistance, and receipt of their paychecks.[8] Additionally, they are oftentimes verbally and physically abused, especially women. Mily describes physical abuse and rape as a normal occurrence for women in the fields, subject to the male crew-leaders that take their pick of the women and then transport them to remote locations on the farm. When surveyed, the majority of women in Lideres Campesinas report being abused physically, emotionally, or both, while working on farms.

Despite their hardships as migrant farm workers, Mily's family relocated to California in 1974 for gainful employment in the fields of the Central Valley. "We would migrate," she says, "to the citrus in Coachella Valley, lemons, grapefruit and oranges, and then to Riverside, where there were many more oranges. Then we would go to Central Valley for almonds and grapes. My brothers would knock down the almonds and my mother and I would be the 'sweepers,' sweeping behind them with rakes." None of the fields that she and her family worked were organic operations, and there was no reprieve from the chemicals in the fields laced with toxic pesticides and herbicides. The sounds of crop planes were omnipresent in the sky as the workers would watch them sweep low and release their poison. Mily remembers the first time it happened to her while in the fields. "I tried to run away; it was terrible. There was sulphur in our eyes and they would get irritated. There were other chemicals that were sprayed that smelled worse. Those experiences and memories will never go away," says Mily, who was joined by other women, some of them pregnant, during the sprayings. Today the negative health impacts of pesticide exposure—including asthma, various cancers, and birth defects in children—are well documented, yet workers continue to be exposed to chemicals and aerial spraying.

The longer Mily worked in the fields, the more her self-confidence diminished. While the verbal abuse and humiliation she experienced mostly came from white male crew leaders and supervisors, such abuse came from Latino co-workers as well. This poor treatment (with little recourse) would continue until Mily's family was introduced to the United Farm Workers (UFW) movement in 1975. Her family became staunch supporters and advocates for fair treatment in the fields and started organizing other families to fight for better wages, bathrooms, health insurance, and field sanitation—all things that they needed and should have rights to. They also pressed companies to ensure no pesticides were sprayed while workers were in the fields, advocating on behalf of their friends and community members. Working as a family team, Mily, her brothers, and her father were able to successfully organize people within the demographics that each of them represented.

"I would talk with other women workers, my brothers would talk to the younger male workers and my father would also help by talking with the older men," she remembers. As a family they were involved in union campaigns—rallying, boycotts, and marching—participated in UFW conferences, and organized at their church. "We believed and fought for our *familia's* wellbeing and the wellbeing of our co-workers, friends, constituents, and others. We always believed in unity and the importance of working together to create change. We had lived in so much exploitation and poverty before this. Asking for a dignified life, asking for fair and livable wages, asking for better treatment, asking for justice and respect made us stronger and united as a community," says Mily.

"A good organizer organizes her family first."

Despite the improvements made by the UFW and their organizing, it was clear to Mily that there was still room for activism and organizing, specifically with women. Mily believes that "a good organizer organizes her family first," and knew that by improving the working conditions for women, their families and communities would also benefit. She and several women did an assessment of thirty farm workers' needs in the Coachella Valley on areas of housing, transportation, social services, and knowledge of English as a second language. This is when they heard many of the women's painful stories from the fields. The need to form a network was apparent to Mily and her fellow interviewers. Together they started Mujeres Mexicanas to address the myriad issues that the women reported as barriers for a healthy life within their communities, schools, and workplaces.

Their next step would be to repeat the outreach in other areas of the Valley. Through the support of Marion Standish at California Rural Legal Assistance (CRLA), conferences were held around the Coachella Valley, growing the movement towards equality for women farm workers and their families. Out of these meetings grew a pressing need to organize in other parts of the state as well, and with support of CRLA, Mily formed Líderes Campesinas in 1992.

> Women, as the center of the family, food preparation, and community, are necessary in creating a more just and fair food system.

Just one year later, the organization held the first ever California-wide conference for farm worker women. It was a huge success. Women traveled from all over the state with their children in tow to talk, listen, celebrate, and mourn their struggles as farm workers and women. With a common history, the women were able to discuss potential solutions to garnering better conditions for farm workers statewide by forming a common alliance based on shared experiences, language, and community culture. The attendees posited that women, as the center of the family, food preparation, and community, are necessarily part of the activating solution in creating a more just and fair food system. This conference extended the reach of Líderes Campesinas to different regions, as far north as Shasta.

Mily epitomizes her belief that women organize their families first, as she raised an activist son, Humberto. "Humberto," says Mily, "is a 'Chicano feminist.' People call him *hijo de la comunidad*. We have a very strong connection and he matured very early because he was involved [in activism] ever since he was in my belly," she smiles. Humberto was given an award for community service when he was only eight years old, the same age Mily was when she started moving irrigation lines in the fields. Through her advocacy, she is working to assure that other children will not have to endure such hard labor and that women will be able to work in safe environments while receiving fair wages.

Today Mily, a widowed single mother, is in the process of earning a graduate school degree while Líderes Campesinas continues strong in twelve regions around the state. This work for social justice is supported by staff, women organizers, volunteers, and youth who continue to fight for improved conditions in the fields and communities throughout California. While she is talking about their fight for basic human rights, she points out that while they are a nonprofit organization officially, their work is not measured by the usual standards of deviation that most networks use. It doesn't matter if there are grants to fund their work—they are fighting for their livelihoods in a profession that needs them. "We really do like to farm," says Mily, speaking for Latino farm workers in California, "and to be outside and working with nature. If the conditions are improved, we will be happy and we will work."

JO ANN BAUMGARTNER

AUTHOR AND DIRECTOR OF WILD FARM ALLIANCE

WFA is responsible for bringing biodiversity conservation to the forefront of organic farming.

On an afternoon in 2007, Jo Ann Baumgartner and her husband, Sam Earnshaw, sat down with two farmer brothers to go over a biodiversity plan for the farm. After they had walked the two through the plan, says Jo Ann, one of them said, "'You know, I always thought nature was my enemy until now.' He was referring to his new perspective about the larger wildlife moving through the corridor from the mountains to the farm's lake edge— that instead of it being a wild, raucous management headache, he then saw that the riparian trees and shrubs breathed with pest-eating birds, bobcats, and coyotes."

Farmers such as these, of large scale and small, are rethinking their stewardship of the land to include environmentally sound practices that support the farm and benefit the wild. They are starting to think about how their land is part of the larger landscape with water and wildlife flowing through.

As director of the Wild Farm Alliance (WFA), Jo Ann knows that change happens when the timing and alignment are right. That advocacy can achieve not just a change in practices but also a transformation of perspective. "WFA is responsible for bringing biodiversity conservation to the forefront of organic farming. Many individual species and whole ecosystems are starting to benefit." The organization was formed in 2000, when sustainable agriculture advocates and conservation proponents came together at the request of the Foundation for Deep Ecology to discuss their often overlooked common commitment to protecting land from development, overexploitation, and urban pollution. At the meeting they discussed the challenges that small and medium-sized farmers face as they practice good stewardship while competing in a globalized food market. Meanwhile, the conservationist calls for wilderness expansion and the restoration of functional ecological connectivity of wildlands. In essence, both need to embrace each other and the larger landscape if the world is to come to terms with the necessity for safe, fresh, and local food, and with the urgency of the biodiversity crisis. WFA emerged from that seminal meeting with a mission to promote a healthy, viable agriculture that protects and restores wild nature.

Before leading WFA, Jo Ann got her hands dirty while farming organically in the '80s and '90s. This has given her a strong basis for helping farmers understand practices that incorporate the natural systems of plant and animal diversity. These systems support a variety of services to the farm—including plantings that provide habitat for predatory insects and hold the soil in place to increase fertility instead of using chemical pesticides and fertilizers. From her previous role as farmer, Jo Ann knows it's possible to move the equation towards more on-farm self-sufficiency while preserving nature and enhancing the farm's business.

Neptune Farm, run by Jo Ann and Sam, had three sites, the largest of which was brimming with wildlife. "We farmed small acreages with wild spaces on them," says Jo Ann. Valuing diversity, she and Sam "wouldn't cut down oak trees in the middle of fields that harbored birds, animals, and insects. We wouldn't kill wildlife, that is, unless they were gophers," she says. (Gophers are notorious for destroying row upon row of vegetable crops and can't easily be kept out of fields.)

As only a farmer can know, growing food in harmony with our wild natural systems has its own challenges. Depending on what someone is farming and where the farm or ranch is located, these challenges can vary from mountain lions

"Wildlife presence on the farm is an indicator of ecosystem health."

snagging sheep to crop invasions by insects, rabbits, or the aforementioned gopher. On their most challenging site, Jo Ann and Sam had to contend with deer and quail. They addressed this by growing varieties that deer didn't eat and by using transplants, instead of direct seeding, which the quail would leave alone. According to Jo Ann, "livestock farmers are addressing the larger challenges through predator-friendly practices. They use guard animals, herd small sheep with large cattle, make unpredictable appearances, and bring vulnerable animals into safety at night." Managing to coexist with those predators means that the farm's rodent population won't skyrocket, and midsized predators in nearby natural landscapes that eat smaller wildlife such as songbirds and lizards will be kept in check.

While many small and diversified farms have incorporated these practices, large farms (those with more than $750,000 in annual sales) are starting to consider how they can lower their off-farm inputs and reduce their bills through these new management practices. From the time between the 2002 and the 2007 census, fertilizer expenses alone increased by 86 percent and fuel costs by 93 percent.[9]

Farms of yesteryear, before chemical agriculture and petroleum, rotated their animal stock to different parcels of the farm and allowed one or more fields to remain fallow any given year for regenerative purposes. Animals were a necessary part of this equation, as they produce all the fertilizer a farm could need: manure, if treated properly, is called black gold for a reason. While in the 1980s farms got a lot of pressure to "Get big or get out!" today we see a slightly different picture. Consolidation of farms is still happening, but we can feel optimistic in that the number of smaller farms is increasing despite the loss of millions of acres of farmland to urbanization, to the tune of 16.2 percent of land between the USDA's 2002 and 2007 Agricultural Censuses.

Farmers are saving money and time using natural systems and are enjoying the results. While nonnative honey bees provide about $17 billion per year worth of pollination services to crops, native pollinators like bumblebees that need natural areas provide $2–$3 billion. In one night, bats can eat their weight in insects, and barn owls, when feeding their young, can capture a dozen rodents. Putting up nesting boxes and interacting with nature is rewarding and can save the time spent applying pesticides.

FARMING WITH THE WILD

Different from the "wild harvested" foods, farming with the wild means taking a few steps back from agriculture's reckless abandonment of our natural systems and calls for a return to the interspecies relationships that co-exist with farming operations. Jo Ann describes farming with the wild as entailing any number of the following activities:

- Creating native bee blocks
- Building bat and owl houses
- Providing a continuous flowering of native plants during the cropping season for beneficial insects
- Conserving water so enough is available for both farming, wildlife, and riparian ecosystems
- Controlling the invasion of introduced species
- Ensuring that contiguous wildlife movement corridors remain intact
- Allowing native plants and animals room to co-exist with a farm
- Not mowing a cover crop all at once in order to preserve beneficial insects on their property (the insects will move to non-mown portions)
- Conserving and restoring the vegetation along riparian areas that helps to filter pathogens and other pollutants and helps to recharge the groundwater
- Practicing "predator friendly" ranching by not killing predators such as coyotes and mountain lions

FOOD SAFETY

Farming with the wild also holds the key to addressing food safety issues. "Food safety as a public health concern is impacting conservation in a huge way in the Salinas Valley," Jo Ann says. "Farmers are being required by shippers and buyers to clear native habitat, which they misguidedly claim will reduce the likelihood of food-borne illnesses such as *E. coli* O157 and salmonella." In reality native wildlife is a low food-safety risk. While cattle are the major reservoirs of *E. coli* O157 on the landscape, non-native feral pigs present a higher risk than native wildlife, and since they did not evolve in the States, they do not use native habitat for cover from predators. Destroying habitat does not lessen their numbers.

    E. coli O157:H7 is perhaps the most well-known food-borne illness in the United States—and for a good reason. Over the past ten years outbreaks and recalls in the nation's food supply have stopped the sales of ground beef, spinach, peanut butter, and peppers. The list goes on, resulting in devastating financial losses for food businesses that are associated with these recalled products. The practice of concentrating thousands of pounds of produce in processing facilities and shipping it all over the country has set the stage for the spread of pathogenic bacteria to the detriment of large numbers of people. As Jo Ann puts it, "It speaks to a broken food system and the need for risky crops like bagged leafy greens to be treated more carefully. Having lots of cut surfaces on the greens, being washed in re-circulated chlorinated water baths, placed in plastic bags, and having a sell date of up to 17 days is riskier than buying a head of lettuce [in a store]." But for the people who want the convenience of eating factory fresh-cut bagged leafy greens, they should only buy it if it has been kept cool and the product's sell date is not close to the end of its range.

What Jo Ann and proponents of biodiversity echo is that the solution does not need to be high tech; it is readily available on each and every farm across the country. "Grasses and wetlands, when left in place, filter *E. coli* pathogens from water, and soils that are highly diverse have a better capacity to break down pathogens in a few days after they are tilled," says Jo Ann. "Now that vegetative edges on farms are being taken out, the Clean Water Act, the Endangered Species Act, the National Organic Program standards, and federal money in the Farm Bill, each working towards conserving our natural resources, are all being compromised," she says. Wild Farm Alliance was invariably drawn into the debate as the "food safety requirements to farm in sterile situations goes against our mission."

FARMERS AS STEWARDS

Despite the risk that food safety poses on sustainable food and farming in America, there have been some positive changes in the last few years that include growing eater interest and recognition at the national level of the role that biodiversity plays in a healthy agriculture and, especially, in organic certification.

Perhaps one of the biggest victories for Jo Ann and her work with the Wild Farm Alliance is the recognition that organic farmers and ranchers have a serious responsibility—not only to produce food, but to work as stewards of our natural spaces.

For six years, Jo Ann worked with organic farmers, certifiers, and the National Organic Standards Board (NOSB) to address the biodiversity conservation requirement in the USDA's National Organic Program. In 2005, the NOSB adopted a whole suit of model inspections questions that certifiers use to address water quality and conservation, creation of wildlife habitat that encourages native pollinators and other beneficial organisms, restoration of natural areas, the control of invasive species, and predator-friendly practices. Culminating with a 2009 NOSB meeting in Washington, D.C., where Jo Ann gave additional testimony, biodiversity is now being comprehensively dealt with—from the organic regulatory arm of the USDA making sure organic certifiers are checking for biodiversity conservation, to farmers themselves ensuring that the soil, water, wetlands, woodlands, and wildlife are maintained or improved. Jo Ann says, "This is a huge win, as previously environmental conservation on a farm was perceived to have no role in determining organic certification. Formerly, an organic farm that valued beneficial organisms providing ecosystem services was the same as one that killed everything that moved." During these meetings the USDA confirmed their commitment to addressing biodiversity and described their plans to incorporate it into their certifier trainings. It's a first important step in their recognition that biological diversity has a place in organic farming.

"Organic farmers are often the innovators in the community, the ones their neighbors watch for new ideas they might want to mimic. Now that they will be spreading the knowledge that conservation is not only good for the environment but good for their farm's bottom line, we may see an improvement over time that stretches beyond the approximately four million acres of organic ground to conventional farmers as well," says Jo Ann.

Ultimately, it will be up to us, the eaters, to show farmers that these practices are worth the effort by buying products that take the natural systems into account, and by giving our support for the most environmentally responsible foods possible.

MELISSA NELSON, PH.D.

AUTHOR, PRESIDENT AND EXECUTIVE DIRECTOR OF THE CULTURAL CONSERVANCY

The Cultural Conservancy works to protect the ancestral lands and cultural traditions of Native peoples of North America, the Pacific, and beyond.

As president and executive director of the Cultural Conservancy, Melissa Nelson and her team work to protect the ancestral lands and cultural traditions of Native peoples of North America, the Pacific, and beyond. As part of this work she helps maintain and restore native food traditions and the cultural practices that accompany indigenous foodways—ways of growing, preserving and cultivating food. This critical work in the preservation of our food traditions and varieties holds untold answers for our future of sustainable food production.

Growing up in rural Mendocino County, California, Melissa felt so much a part of the forests and rivers of the land she lived on. "I was part of an undivided wholeness. This connection to place was visceral and spiritual, not intellectual; it seems to be something innate when one is blessed with growing up in a healthy natural environment."

As an enrolled member of the Turtle Mountain Band of Chippewa Indians of North Dakota, Melissa is of mixed-blood heritage: Chippewa (Anishinaabe) and French-Cree (Métis) from her mother, and Norwegian from her father. At age twenty-five, she was doing environmental education work in the Pacific Northwest when she read about the work of the Cultural Conservancy. Inspired by the organization's mission and the sacred site work of one of its main founders, Claire Hope Cummings (see Chapter 2), she contacted the nonprofit organization to find a way to get involved. After proving her commitment to the cause, she was honored to take on a leadership role with the Conservancy. "I was elated to find and work for an organization that was so aligned with my life passion and core values of indigenous rights, spiritual connection to place, and protection of native biodiversity," Melissa remembers.

By serving as executive director of the organization since 1993, she has been working with the mission of the organization to renew Native ways of connecting to the natural world. By incorporating indigenous ecological insights and practices from native origins, histories, and worldviews, Melissa demonstrates that Native peoples need to be respected and consulted on all levels of environmental management and decision-making. "Due to the history of injustice and oppression, tribes and Native communities today need a lot of support in protecting their lands, waters, and traditional lifestyles," she says. "Their teachings and practices are not about romanticizing the past but are very relevant for ecological planning and social justice today."

"Native teachings and practices are not about romanticizing the past but are very relevant for ecological planning and social justice today."

CULTIVATING THE WILD

Preceding the local food movement in the U.S. by thousands of years, growing, cultivating, hunting, collecting, and "wild tending" of the land was a basic practice of indigenous peoples living with an intimate understanding of the natural cycles of the seasons. The abundant wild and semi-wild fruits, vegetables, nuts, seeds, and grains all contributed to tribes' vibrantly healthy diets. Wild game, fish, and seafood also added to the health of the native diet. This native science and practice still survives among many elders and the traditional food practitioners of today. Their biggest challenge to practicing these traditions is in finding natural, "wild" places, as well as the remnant historic gardens and lands, that can be accessed by tribal members. Lands clean and safe from pollution and that have the native resources available for wild tending are becoming more scarce.

These practices of wild tending allowed many species of plants and animals to co-evolve with humans. The Coast Miwok Indians of Northern California provide an example of how natives co-evolved with the clams and seafood of the northern California shores. Prior to the National Park System's involvement in coastal management, the tribe had successfully cultivated clam and oyster beds over generations.

Their practices helped cull and thin the populations so that they would continue producing abundantly. With the removal of their rights to do so by the parks service, the clams and oysters fell into decline as the beds became overcrowded and food resources scarce. This is just one of many such examples of the symbiotic and balancing relationships humans still have with the natural cycles among Earth's wild creatures. While many of us may feel disconnected from this interrelationship today, we still play a very strong role in the survivability of numerous species through our day-to-day food choices.

WOMEN'S ROLE IN WILD CULTIVATION

As an activist with the Conservancy and professor of American Indian Studies at San Francisco State University, Melissa has conducted extensive interviews in the United States and Canada about Native American women's roles in food production. "Women were often the lead in food planting and gathering, and they held important leadership roles within tribes," says Melissa. Women and clan mothers of the Mohawk, for example, controlled the planting, production and storage of crops. But when the colonial forces and then the U.S. government came in, "they told the men that they needed to be the farmers, not the women, and it completely disrupted traditional gender roles," says Melissa. By relocating tribes to marginal lands, the government changed tribal languages, customs, cultural identities, and diets. Adding insult to injury, the tribes were then forced to accept low-quality commodity foods from the government.

These foods were never meant to replace staple food items, but because Native Americans were forced onto marginal lands where they could not grow or collect traditional foods, the supplements became the mainstay. Commodity foods are still distributed through the U.S. government's Food Distribution Program for Indian Reservations, although the offerings have improved substantially. Monthly food packages are still provided to approximately 243 tribes throughout the United States. Melissa

"Women were often the lead in food planting and gathering, and they held important leadership roles within tribes."

states that more than half of tribe populations suffer from diabetes due to western diets of processed foods, white flour products, sugar and high fructose corn syrup. These adverse health conditions are quickly reversed when people go back to their native food diets.[10]

In order to encourage more tribal members to eat more healthfully, tribal women must be re-empowered and supported in growing the traditional foods that their bodies, their very genes, are accustomed to. The same rings true of people of other ethnicities such as Latinos, African Americans, and others living in the processed food climes of the United States. The traditional Native American "three sisters" garden exemplifies the wisdom of native food knowledge: corn stands tall for beans to grow on, beans fix nitrogen in the soil, and squash shades out weeds—providing staple nutrition for both people and the land. These "three sisters" combined to form a balanced diet of carbohydrates, essential fats, and protein long before modern science even identified these nutrients. The intuitive and learned agronomy and horticultural skills that indigenous people have practiced over the centuries hold infinite solutions to challenges such as drought and diversity.

> Tribal women must be re-empowered and supported in growing the traditional foods that their bodies are accustomed to.

Melissa has found that oral traditions such as song and storytelling have been the primary way to pass down knowledge between tribal members for thousands of years, including information about food and the land. As a collaborative ethnographer, Melissa has been recording the songs, stories, and thus histories of these Native American communities across the United States, including Hawaii, such as "The Salt Song Trail" recordings. It is critical to document and protect invaluable traditional teachings about herb lore, hunting and fishing, and gathering wild and cultivated fruits, vegetables, and grains; about how to return to a more holistic relationship with the other species of our planet; how to give thanks to the plants and animals, the soil that grows our food, and for water that is clean. This reverence for the beauty and bounty of nature is a vital part of the solution to global climate change and our environment's regeneration.

RECIPES FOR ACTION

The following are a list of ideas so that you—as an eater, a farmer, or a food business—can get involved in the networks promoting environmentally minded food systems. These are just some thoughts on how to get involved; an expansive list of books and organizations are in the "Resources" section.

EATER

As an eater, you play a role in supporting sustainable agriculture networks. Here's how you can plug in:

- Join or volunteer for the organization of your choice that's working to support what you are most interested in regarding the food system. Or consider giving a donation.
- Attend Farm Aid, a fun annual music festival whose proceeds directly benefit family farmers.
- Host a fundraiser or mixer at your house to raise awareness and/or money for an organization.
- If you're really into an issue—labor, environment, native foods, etc.—you may want to start a blog about it.
- Buy food from as close to home as possible: shop at farmers markets, buy locally produced dairy products, nuts, honey, and meats. Buy native and fairly traded foods as often as you can.

FARMER

As a farmer, your work providing food is the foundation for our community. You can further engage in the issues by:

- Working with the United Farm Workers or Agricultural Justice Project to implement a progressive farm labor policy on your farm.
- Plant hedgerows for beneficial insects.
- Join a sustainable farming organization in your area.
- Host an on-farm event to engage your community.
- Attend meetings to represent the voice of agriculture in critical local government discussions.

FOOD BUSINESS

Businesses play an important role in supporting local and regional food systems that promote diversity, sustainability, and community. There are numerous ways that businesses can take action to support and help preserve family farms:

- Partner with a community organization to hold fundraisers.
- Offer your Public Health Department–certified kitchen to farmers for processing their goods. Put these products on your menu or sell them in your store.
- Be a host site for a CSA farm or a farmers market.
- Implement a food-marketing program in your business that promotes foods that are local, organic, and native.
- Give incentives to your customers to support local organizations. You can give people an opportunity to donate money in addition to their bill. Or you can host a community day, where local sustainable food networks are invited to do outreach to educate your patrons.
- Some businesses will choose a day to donate a percentage of their proceeds (such as 5 percent) to select organizations. This provides great publicity for both the business and the organization and builds broader community support as the organization will outreach to their constituents.
- Some businesses offer a rebate for customers who bring their own reuseable bags for shopping. These bag rebates can be offered to sustainable agriculture organizations.

URBAN FARM WOMEN

W hile smaller in size than their rural counterparts, what urban farms and gardens lack in acreage, they make up for in density and impact on our urban population. People in urban areas might run a CSA, provide fresh food to a food bank, or grow subsistence gardens important for preserving food and cultural traditions. They often provide educational opportunities for children (big and small), sell the food to local food businesses, train people how to run a small produce business, or host workshops, potlucks or speakers on the subject of food. Urban farms and gardens are usually a combination of business and education. This chapter does not cover community gardens, which are primarily for those who want to grow their own.

With 80 percent of Americans living in cities, the reintegration of food production right where the majority of people live, work, and play is one of the best ways to rebuild our appreciation for local foods.[1] While farms and gardens used to be integrated into city urban planning, real estate prices forced farmers farther and farther away from the urban core. It is imperative that urban planners and city representatives be reengaged in the process, as farming vegetables on urban land has a greater value than its residential zoning designation illustrates.

When I talk about the growth in bolstering our urban farms and gardens to connect more people to the source of their food, I'm not talking about supplanting rural production; we need the quantity of food that rural places provide. And while urban farms could grow tons of produce each and every year, these farms are filling other niches. After all, there are food jobs to be created, food waste to turn into compost, veggies to be redistributed to people that need them, and the basic experiences of digging, weeding, planting and harvesting to be had.

Thousands of pounds of food could be effectively produced on abandoned lots and even publicly maintained spaces (such as greenways between streets and in parks) while reducing the miles our food has to travel to get from farm to plate. Where there is no land, or in places where the soil is contaminated from industrial waste, built containers and planter boxes on porches or on roofs can suffice. (In the latter scenario, rooftop gardens can reduce energy costs by keeping buildings cool during summertime.)

But urban farms and gardens aren't without their challenges. As our protagonists of this chapter point out, city ordinances may impede farming from happening within city limits, such as the bans on composting urban waste, recycling water, or keeping chickens in many towns. While many of these out-of-date regulations were created when people needed to be more concerned about the spread of disease, today we need to recapture and reuse our resources as wisely as possible. While the learning curve for our city officials may be uphill before they get behind farms and gardens that seek to use techniques such as methane digesters (gas from compost) to heat greenhouses, or put a garden on a vacant lot or roadway, the women in this chapter are starting the dialogue. When the women here pair their activities with job training programs, urban farms act as hubs for education that promote economic, environmental, and food sustainability. This is how we can address food justice in our communities—by giving people access to culturally appropriate foods.

Our older generations still remember the skills and times when people were more food savvy, frugal, and creative. When I lived on a small plot in West Berkeley, on a fairly run-down part of Sixth Street, our yard had a vegetable garden, chickens, and a great big wild plum tree. I remember one day when I was out back and a woman up on the second story yelled down, "Hey! Do you mind if I come down and pick some of those plums?" For the next half hour I listened to her talk about canning the plums like her grandma would do. When we are able to reconnect with nature in our urban environments we get in touch with our past, our soil and the seasonal diversity that brings not only freshness, but a deeper commitment and connection to the community in which we live.

ERIKA ALLEN

CHICAGO PROJECTS MANAGER, GROWING POWER

Growing Power is an organization that works to provide urban residents with job training and access to healthy, fresh, affordable food.

It's winter in Chicago and the earth is a frozen mass, up to twenty or more feet down. Below the soil of the city's urban parks, spring's coming attractions lay dormant. No food can be grown here except for spinach and other cool weather crops in hoop houses. It's during this down time that Erika Allen plans for fruit and vegetable production as well as the educational programming of the three urban farm sites she manages in downtown Chicago.

Erika's story of starting Growing Power Chicago began with her upbringing on her family's farm just outside of Milwaukee's city limits and in the greenhouses of Growing Power Milwaukee that her dad, Will Allen, started. With a living classroom on Silver Spring Drive, Erika worked in the greenhouse throughout her adolescence, helping lead tours of the 35,000 visitors that came through every year. She also watered plants, fed the fish, and turned compost. While she didn't always love these chores as a teenager and early twenty-something, she inherently gained invaluable life skills— skills she is working to give today's youth the opportunity to learn.

GROWING POWER MILWAUKEE

When you walk into the first of six greenhouses, you can smell the compost decaying. The exterior glass walls are steamed over from humidity created by the massive fish tanks in Greenhouse Five. Every inch is crammed with the twenty thousand plants, from sprouts to microgreens, that are feeding local residents. The greens that they sprout throughout the year are a godsend for those who wish to eat fresh and locally during Wisconsin's cold winters, when local food options are limited to meat, cheese and root vegetables. The two-acre farm and greenhouse site is the last remaining farm in the city of Milwaukee, although Will Allen still runs his family farm just outside of the city limits. This farm also grows some food and acts as the primary supplier of compost for the Chicago and Milwaukee urban operations. At the farm, they also host a variety of educational opportunities for youth and immigrant farmers.

"Racism, oppression, and food justice— these are all interconnected."

Just as Erika and her brother have grown up with farming in their blood, co-director Karen Parker has been at Growing Power Milwaukee from day one—since 1993, when Will decided to open his city greenhouses to grow food for the community. Will brought Karen over from her previous job as general manager for a nearby Kentucky Fried Chicken. Living adjacent to Growing Power's greenhouses and Community Food Center, where food is sold, distributed and grown, Karen has noticed some changes over the past sixteen years. In addition to her improved eating habits and those of her kids, local residents now have increased access to fresh and culturally appropriate foods and have started to grow their own. "We have more people doing their own growing . . . [it seems every-body] is doing gardens and growing their own vegetables. They get tips from us and get their plants and other things at a discounted rate. It has an impact," she says. Karen has learned over the years to appreciate the freshness of the foods she has access to and is a strong advocate for helping community members change their lives in this way too. "I love the farm because what it means to me is how important farmers are to us," she says, emphasizing the simple fact that farmers are the ones who provide us with one of the basic necessities of life. Karen is part of the new farm stand Growing Power is setting up in another community with limited access to fresh and affordable foods. She'll help duplicate the model they created on Silver Springs Drive, and will offer similar foods—fresh fruits and vegetables, naturally raised chicken, honey, and other essentials—not available through the community's liquor stores (where the majority of the community shops). Major grocery stores have periodically moved out of low-income areas throughout America and have left residents with diminished options for buying food. With limited transportation, a trip to a real grocery store is often too difficult and time intensive.

FARMING FOR COMMUNITY

As a multigenerational African American family farmer, Erika set aside growing food for a couple of years while studying art therapy in Chicago but eventually came back to her roots. While the words "you'll thank me for it" from her father may have sounded like a threat in her youth, she's happy to have learned how to farm and to teach others how to be able to feed themselves, an experience she feels is deeply rewarding.

After Erika finished her bachelor of fine arts and her master's in art therapy in Chicago, she decided to stay in the city. Her first job was with a nonprofit family resource organization where she helped provide an entire cache of services to low-income families in need, one of those needs being food. The Milwaukee Market Basket Program of Growing Power has been growing over the years in providing fresh fruits, vegetables, and eggs to residents in need on a weekly basis. And while Erika's organization made really judicious decisions about what they ordered from the government food commodity programs, she knew they could do better. "I was thinking it would be great to have these Market Baskets next to the commodity food that we provided to them," she says, "so they would have access to more fresh options." While Erika was able to bring in fresh food while she was there, the families also received assistance from other federally supported nutrition programs.

The last Farm Bill allocated $10.4 billion dollars to food assistance programs—a whopping 64 percent of the bill's total allocation. Food banks and other food assistance programs largely do not receive this funding and function like other nonprofits, by applying for grants. It is primarily allocated through the Women Infant and Children (WIC) and Food Stamp (SNAP) programs[2] (see more about the Farm Bill in chapter 2). As Erika points out, if some of this Farm Bill money was redirected toward providing people with more fresh foods via programs such as Growing Power, and if the money worked to teach people how to achieve their own food independence, then we would start seeing some systemic changes in the health and well-being of our most at-risk communities.

GROWING POWER CHICAGO

While working to get more fresh fruit and vegetable offerings to the families she worked with, Erika reconnected with the work she was immersed in before art school—that of food and community. Her dad invited her to the Illinois Food Security Conference in spring of 2001. "That was it for me," she says, in reference to coming back to food. "All of the dots lined up," and by February of 2002, she had opened the Chicago Growing Power office. "Food is the next frontier in social justice, and working in food is a great way to help transform how people are living in Chicago," she says.

When she first opened Growing Power Chicago's doors, she didn't realize how difficult it would be. Her desire to bring Growing Power to Chicagoans was met with resistance due to existing organizations' territorial issues and institutional racism from people that weren't used to working with people of color. The organizations working on food issues, according to Erika, had received funding for years but weren't really achieving their proposed results. So when Erika opened the Growing Power office on a mission to grow food and provide jobs and youth training programs, her efforts were met with skepticism. "People admire what you're doing, but you're kind of blowing the lid off of what they've been saying they were going to do. So it's this weird combination of admiration and mild hatred," she says.

Sexism and racism have also proven to be a challenge in her work and that of her colleagues, despite Chicago's racial diversity. Erika has been keenly aware of the general lack of color at the city council meetings and in other nonprofit organizations working on food access. "I am a woman of color, and that has been challenging at times. I work with a lot of women but not a lot of women of color," she says. This is another fundamental difference with Growing Power's multicultural staff; they are more representative of the communities that they serve, making them a truly grassroots organization. Erika notes that at times it can be challenging for them to work with outside organizations and the predominantly white city officials, as there are both cultural and racial divides. "Just our confidence and ability to challenge things becomes a barrier. People (meaning white folks) aren't used to that; they're used to being the experts and being in the place of expertise rather than getting information from a person of color, especially a woman." Despite these challenges, Erika remains strong. "I have a high degree of education and can talk about this stuff all the good long day." She's also extremely patient, a skill of tolerance that she claims to have been coached on by her father.

To counter the feelings of institutionalized racism in the food and sustainable agriculture community, Erika helped start a group called the Growing Food and Justice Initiative (GFJI), which is proactively creating community for people of color. "It's been really amazing to work on issues without institutional barriers within the organization," she says. GFJI meets annually and works to address racism, oppression, and food justice. "These are all interconnected," says Erika. She is convinced that as long as people of color lack access to healthy and culturally appropriate foods, true food security will not be achieved.

After seven years in the Chicago community, things are getting to be a bit easier for Erika and her team. "At this point everyone knows who we are. I don't have to justify everything that we do. Before, there were many incredulous faces when we talked about growing [food] on asphalt," she says with a smile.

BENEFITS OF FARMS TO URBAN AREAS

After the risk of frost is over, sometime in mid-May, and the wind has stopped sweeping snow and below-freezing winds from the north, Erika, her volunteers, and a group of urban youth start planting vegetables and other annuals on the three urban farm sites on city-owned parks. These farms will feed and inspire the community throughout the growing season with fresh produce, aesthetic green spaces, community activities, and educational programs designed to engage youth.

Erika is convinced that urban farming in areas that need the access to food and jobs the most allows for "an integrated approach to addressing food security, as well as ecological, nutrition and public health issues."

One of Growing Power Chicago's farm sites is located in Cabrini Green, a redeveloped housing project on Chicago's North Side. For many years the project had a reputation for drug dealing and violence and exemplified public housing problems around the country. The Cabrini Green farm is giving residents a new opportunity to achieve food independence while learning job skills and training by growing, distributing, and selling these foods. Located at the intersection of West Chicago Avenue and North Hudson Avenue, the farm is a gem of hope for the area's residents. With her background, Erika is reconstructing the concept of urban farms.

Erika has applied her artistic eye to all of the Growing Power sites, the most public one being the Grant Park Farm. With twenty thousand square feet on the scenic lake front, the farm boasts well over 150 heirloom veggies, edible flowers, and herbs. It has a great location and is easily accessible for educational opportunities for local youth, such as planting, harvesting, learning about the nutrient cycles of food systems, and composting. Erika is determined to use her aesthetic understanding to change the reputation of these urban farms so they are more appealing and attractive to the general public. "When you're trying to change how people perceive agriculture, you want to present it in an appealing environment," she says.

Growing Power's other farm, Jackson Park Urban Farm and Community Allotment Garden, grows food on a half-acre of land supplying Chicago's South Side with fresh produce. Raised beds, trainings, community outreach, and education all occur here on site as well. Jackson Park uses the "worm system approach," a tool developed by Growing Power to teach people about closed-loop nutrient systems, from food scraps to compost and back into food. While this cycle is critical to creating sustainable cities of the future, Erika has felt frustrated that the city has yet to allow Growing Power to compost urban waste for use on the farm. "As we move forward and hit our goals and benchmarks, still, our biggest challenge is compost," says Erika. After several years of operation, they still truck their compost in from Milwaukee, a two-hour drive (depending on traffic) from her family's farm (the Merton farm) located just north of the city. "We can't compost on a large scale in the city to provide for our needs. This is one of the educational policy issues we're working on," says Erika.

Erika's mission to be self-sufficient within the city of Chicago and provide the food and entrepreneurial skills possible within an urban food system have led her to focus mainly on youth. "We've really worked a lot with youth and bringing them into this project by teaching them a whole host of life skills and teaching them some of the foundational things of where their food comes from and how to grow it," she says. She knows that through their work they're not only increasing youth's chances of being healthier adults, but also providing them with opportunities to develop the "boundaries and coping mechanisms" skills that some of the city's youth need the most. Erika finds this a really rewarding endeavor and is enthusiastic about "creating a career track, that if the kids were plopped down somewhere with a sack of seeds [and Growing Power is successful] they could raise food for themselves."

ZONING LAWS AND OTHER CHALLENGES

Zoning laws, composting regulations, and understanding at the city level about the potential of urban farms to grow food, make compost, and generate electricity, are just a few of Erika's hurdles when it comes to making the three farm sites work both spatially and economically. Since 2002, Erika has served as a co-chair of the Chicago Food Policy Advisory Council to create recommendations for policy change that could swing their work in a whole new direction. According to the group's mission, "The Chicago Food Policy Advisory Council (CFPAC) will facilitate the development of responsible policies that improve access for Chicago residents to culturally appropriate, nutritionally sound, and affordable food that is grown through environmentally sustainable practices." The Community Food Security Coalition has a list of eighty similar food policy councils on their website that span the United States, including Native American and Canadian councils (see Recipes for Action).

If she could wave a magic wand, perhaps her biggest policy change would be to change the zoning laws in Chicago to create "agricultural" distinctions. Without it, the value of the land when classified as urban use is too expensive for farming. (One tomato, for example, if grown on "residentially zoned land" would be worth thousands of dollars.) The good news is that since the city has zoning distinctions for "parks," "forest," and "cemetery" land, certainly it can create new food and agriculture designations.

"We're not policy makers," says Erika, "we're practitioners who are working hard for the land. We don't want just community gardens but real city farms where we can take policy-makers and people in the community through the educational process, so they understand the potential." Erika would love to see the Chicago branch of Growing Power "get a large tract of land, be able to grow a lot of food, and also be able to host micro food enterprises and do green job trainings. We want to be big enough so it's not just window dressing." She wants to grow the urban farms into "serious production and provide some jobs as well as energy by incorporating anaerobic digesters on a large scale." These digesters take composting material and capture the methane (natural gas) that can be used for heating or cooking instead of contributing to global warming. If Erika can get it approved by the city, she'll be able to efficiently heat her greenhouses in the wintertime for free. These digesters could also eventually provide heat and energy outside of their operation, to other Chicagoans.

Through her work, Erika presents us with the solutions and is opening the dialogue of how equality, food production, and food security go hand in hand. For her, it's been a point of personal and professional growth dovetailing the two curricula of farming and art to building greater food security for Chicago's three million residents— especially for those that need it the most.

WILLOW ROSENTHAL

AUTHOR AND
FOUNDER, CITY
SLICKER FARMS

City Slicker Farms is
a collection of urban
farm plots that grows
food on abandoned lots
for urban residents.

Willow Rosenthal hails from Graton, California, an hour north of San Francisco, where dairies, fruit growers, and fisheries still predominate in the landscape. Rolling green hills stretch out to the Pacific, where oyster fisheries dot the coastline. Growing up in this environment, she witnessed the impact that farming has on our everyday lives. "It really influenced me," she says, "and I always felt motivated by the injustices growing up, even in a rural farming community." She was especially disturbed when she learned as a child that the people who worked the hardest—the farm workers—seemed to be the poorest. She also grew up with a strong connection to the history of the tribes (Pomo and Ohlone) and people that planted so many seeds of abundance. She, too, loved to garden, a skill and appreciation that she learned from her father, who "transmitted his love of gardening" to her. While in high school her favorite pastimes were gardening, canning, cooking for her family, and working at Foggy Bottom Farm in Graton, founded by her mentor, Anna Ransom. Anna impressed upon her that farming was a possible path, but it was Willow that would bring justice into the mix years later, ensuring that the people that needed food the most could access it.

If you live in Northern California and have an interest in food and sustainable farming, the lure of the Bay Area beckons you constantly. As if the heavy concentration of nonprofits working on sustainable food isn't enough, there's the ultra-hip food industry that lures chefs, foodies, and educators alike. In 1997, Willow was officially pulled in for an internship with Food First, an international think tank that focuses on workers' rights and social justice in relation to food, located in Oakland. She also volunteered with the Organic Consumers Association (OCA) and the International Society for Ecology and Culture (ISEC).

The OCA advocates for the integrity of organic food standards on behalf of consumers and the food industry. While the OCA was doing good work, the organization's scope was too narrow for Willow's concerns. She wanted the organic farming community to start talking about low-income food access and workers' rights. "I debated going into farming myself," says Willow, "but I knew I would be a farmer and sell at the farmers markets to rich people." Instead, she moved to one of the biggest food deserts in Oakland.

When Willow moved to West Oakland, she had to travel several miles to Berkeley Bowl, a store with a cult-like following, to buy sustainably grown foods. During these excursions she thought about what a food desert West Oakland was, with only one grocery store to serve twenty-three thousand residents. (More affluent areas average one grocery store per four thousand residents.) Food that is sold is largely processed junk food easily accessible in any one of the liquor stores—one per every six hundred twenty-five residents—with only a handful (three or four) that carry any sort of fresh fruits or vegetables.[3]

According to a 1998 Oakland Food Assessment, the food sold in the community's fifty liquor stores is oftentimes 30 to 100 percent more expensive than food sold in full-service grocery stores.[4] This leads many of the residents to rely on the numerous emergency food provision sites throughout the community—an important indicator that a community has food access issues. This report sums up the disparity that similar low-income communities are facing across the United States: "Living on the margins, the community of West Oakland faces compounding barriers that significantly impact the health of its 23,000 urban residents. Studies show that the interconnected stresses of poverty, pollution, lack of transportation, and limited access to healthy food lead West Oakland residents to suffer disproportionately with higher rates of diabetes and toxic chemical exposure, all of which lead to severe health problems and reduced life expectancy."[5] In the Oakland Unified

"There really is a way to reconnect to the people and places where our food comes from, and that's the big underlying theme with all of my work—how to make the connection."

School District, for example, an estimated one-third of students will suffer from diabetes in their lifetime due to their diets and levels of physical activity.[6]

While it was once Oakland's booming shopping and industrial zone with the Port of Oakland nearby, today the residents, 80 percent people of color, are some of the poorest in the Bay Area. The landscape consists mostly of industrial leftovers—polluted brownfields that pose problems to growing food directly in the soil.[7] Just one example of "environmental injustice" where disadvantaged, low-income communities live in toxic places because they have no other choice—they can't afford to move to more affluent, less-polluted neighborhoods, and the need to focus on daily necessities makes advocating for political change difficult.

It was 1998 and Willow was noticing an awful lot of unused and abandoned lots in the area, what urban planners refer to as *urban blight*—tires, junk, and who knows what else under the soil. "What if West Oakland could grow its own food right here?" she thought. The idea of farming in Oakland and of providing food for the community kept coming to her mind. She started discussing this prospect with people in the neighborhood and through a chance conversation with a local realtor, she learned about the county's annual tax defaulted land auction. A friend offered to loan her some money to go to the auction, and after much research and biking around the neighborhood, she succeeded in purchasing an empty lot for $11,000. This was the beginning of City Slicker Farms.

Urban farms vary in size and shape, and it's unclear what makes one urban food production site a "farm" and another a "garden." The United States Department of Agriculture (USDA) defines a farm as "any place from which $1,000 or more of agricultural products were produced and sold, or normally would have been sold, during the census year."[8] This quantifying system, however, falls short of assessing the value local food production and the preservation of the land and soil offers a community.

"I call it 'market gardening' and determine its value more by the methods that are used, not by whether it's a cooperative, a collective, a for-profit, or a nonprofit, or even that it makes a profit," she says. Her main determination of whether the City Slicker plots are small farms or gardens depends on whether or not animals are present to close the energy loop by providing fertilizer. In the ten years since City Slicker Farms began, it has created six urban farm plots ranging from the size of a backyard to a quarter-acre. City Slicker Farms' sites are run as "market farms," producing as much food as possible in small spaces. Willow used the techniques she learned in the commercial farming sector to change the idea of "community gardening" to "community farming"—rather than growing mixed beds of flowers and vegetables, City Slicker Farms' sites grow thousands of pounds a year of subsistence food crops.

The social and environmental returns, incalculable by our economy, far surpass any monetary values that would be associated with a bunch of the farms' carrots. Their Center Street farm, for example, opened in 2000, and has been transformed with the help of West Oaklanders. With just over 3,800 square feet (.08 of an acre), they are able to keep chickens, ducks, beehives, compost piles, habitat for wildlife and beneficial insects, an outdoor kitchen, a wood-fired oven, and a workshop space. This site hosts a weekly farm stand where local residents can buy produce on a donation basis or—get this—access the food for free. They've found that over the years even the poorest residents generally want to pay something for their food and are very grateful to be able to buy fresh, seasonal fruits and vegetables. Urban farms have more social capital than the money they make, but as Willow justifies, "Making money isn't the point." After years of trial and error and perfecting the urban approach to growing food, City Slicker Farms' urban farms now serve the community that the project set out to impact. The six sites are run and managed by the organization's two paid staff, along with volunteers, interns, three full-time apprentices and local residents who help maintain beds and cultivate the food.

In 2008 alone, City Slicker diverted twenty tons of waste from the landfill, created ten tons

> The social and environmental returns of urban farming far surpass any monetary values.

of compost, propagated over fourteen thousand plants, and distributed eight thousand pounds of produce through the farm stand. More than half of that was grown on their urban sites on fractions of acres— one-eighth of an acre here, another one there—spread throughout West Oakland.[9]

HELPING PEOPLE GROW THEIR OWN FOOD

In 2005, as demand for produce increased and the difficulty of getting access to land became clear, Willow decided to start a new program within City Slicker Farms: the Backyard Garden Program. Willow had noticed that while community members flocked to the urban farm sites to stock up on produce, the farm stand customers—working people— didn't necessarily have time to work in the garden. She had a suspicion that by supplying people with the materials and information needed to grow food in their own yards, they would be much more likely to find time to garden. With large African American and Hispanic populations, the community already had a wealth of knowledge about growing food, but what soon became clear was that people lacked access to the material resources needed to get the gardens growing. Buying materials at a garden center cancelled out any savings from growing food, and it was often too much work for an individual to raise healthy seedlings in a windowsill or try to find cheap or free compost.

The Backyard Garden Program was designed to fill in the gaps so people could grow their own high-quality, nutritious produce and share it with their community. Since 2005, a crew of City Slicker Farms staff and volunteers has shown up almost every Saturday at a community member's house with a truck full of compost, already constructed planter boxes and trellises, tools, a fruit tree, plants, and seeds. Through a prior assessment visit, the crew already knows who in the family can help build and maintain the garden, what vegetables are preferred, and if the soil is safe for gardening. Within four hours, a back or front yard is transformed into a food-producing garden complete with wood planter boxes, mulched paths, and new seedlings. After the garden is built, a mentor provides information on how to tend the garden and checks in with the family every few months. After two years of mentoring, the family gains unlimited access to supplies that they pick up themselves at the City Slicker Farms nursery.

The success of the Backyard Garden Program led Willow to begin working to implement policies that would allow the program to eventually be available to all Oakland residents and, hopefully, expand throughout the state. To create a foundation to scale up the work, Willow helped write the Oakland Food Systems Assessment and organized her community to lobby the Oakland City Council to start a Food Policy Council that could, in the future, implement strategies to improve food access in all Oakland neighborhoods. She also began to work with the city to create a model private/public collaboration to turn a city park into an urban farm with funding from city and private sources. She also learned that the government of Venezuela was implementing a similar strategy on a national basis and went on a fact-finding tour to learn how best to scale up such a program locally.

Many of City Slicker Farms' methods, such as hiring community members to mentor new participants, and creating central supply sites like greenhouses and gardening material hubs, were being utilized in Venezuela as well; so Willow knew she was on the right track. It was inspiring for her to see that it could be done on a much larger scale. In 2009 City Slicker Farms built its hundredth backyard garden, now a model throughout the country.

TAKING THE PROGRAMS BEYOND OAKLAND

While Willow has turned over the reigns of City Slicker Farms to a new set of leaders, she continues designing programs in other parts of the Bay Area. Through City Slicker Farms as her umbrella organization, Willow provides consulting to other organizations and government agencies on program design, funding, maintenance, and evaluation, as well as guides projects through the initial design and build phase. One of her most notable projects was helping install the Victory Garden in 2008 in front of San Francisco City Hall. As a part of the Slow Food Nation conference, Willow collaborated with a few others (including Amy Franchescini, John Bela, Garden for the Environment, and volunteers) to design, build, plant and maintain the victory garden. This garden, plush with vegetables and sustainable materials, carried the support from city officials and represented a new opening to garner the support of the city for urban food production.

Recently, Willow designed a one-acre urban farm for the San Francisco Job Corps training program that will serve the site's culinary and building trades programs and expose hundreds of low-income youth to the concept of sustainable farming.

In the future, Willow hopes to help City Slicker Farms bring its backyard farming strategy to the State of California through collaborating with federal and state programs, especially the Food Stamp Program and the University of California Cooperative Extension. She believes that to create a successful urban farming sector it's important to harness and redirect the powers inherent in our current government infrastructure to serve the needs of the people—like they were created to do. The private nonprofit sector can't do it alone. Willow never thought she would achieve so much from a simple idea of buying an abandoned lot and looks forward to supporting others in their beginnings—one step at a time.

NOVELLA CARPENTER

AUTHOR AND
URBAN FARMER,
GHOST TOWN
FARM, OAKLAND,
CALIFORNIA

Ghost Town Farm is a
vegetable and meat farm
near downtown Oakland.

CO-OWNER,
BIOFUEL OASIS

Biofuel Oasis is a
veggie-oil/diesel gas
station in Berkeley.

The buzzing of the 980 freeway and the swish of BART trains compete with the car alarms and troublemaking that happens in Novella Carpenter's Oakland, California, neighborhood. This is not the bright and shiny vision one might be used to when thinking of a DIY farm, but Ghost Town Farm is a site that is producing honest-to-goodness food. Pushing the limits of urban survivalism, Novella never dreamed she would have this much land to play with.

Novella and her boyfriend, Bill, were eager to have the lot next door when it went up for sale. "But they were asking like $450,000 for 4,500 square feet. It was totally ridiculous, but at that time there was mad land-grabbing going on in Oakland," she says. The woman who ended up buying the land told Novella that she "loves roses and daylilies" and that Novella could grow anything she wanted "as long as it wasn't illegal." Luckily for Novella, the landlady has never come around with a development proposal, since real estate has crashed.

Novella and Bill went to work right away cutting through the jungle that had overgrown the lot. Below all the weeds and rubble was a circular patch of dirt that she had a friend test for heavy metals before even thinking about planting. When the results came back negative, she was on her way to being a proper vegetable squatter.

Squatting on unused urban land, free of rent, always had an appeal to Novella. First thing she planted corn, then came the chickens and the bees, and it went a little wild from there.

"My neighbors still think I'm crazy," says Novella. She undoubtedly received some special recognition at the post office when picking up boxes that were buzzing and peeping. The rotating collection of animals has included turkeys, geese, goats, two pigs (now dry-curing at a restaurant), and ducks, in addition to vegetables and other plant-based edibles.

When Novella is not weeding or tending to her flock, she's blogging about their intrepidness or writing for numerous Bay Area and national magazines and newspapers. In her memoir, *Farm City*, she humorously describes how she ate exclusively from the plot for an entire month with only minor repercussions. Her experimentation of being an extreme locavore lost her a few pounds *and* a few chickens, but overall she found that with the right preparation and timing, it could be done—even without coffee. Even her neighbors have started to show some interest.

Novella's neighbors have been really lenient thus far, despite the barnyard she has going out back. With the workshop and tour guests traipsing through the shuttered and cluttered neighborhood, if a neighbor complains, she takes a "no tolerance" policy. "We live in the hood and there's shooting and car alarms," Novella says, "but once we had a turkey that gobbled incessantly, incessantly, incessantly. My neighbor said, 'That turkey gobbles every hour.' 'I know,' " she said to the neighbor, " 'I'm taking care of him right now.' If the neighbors complain, off with the turkeys' heads."

Biofuel Oasis

Since 2005, Novella's day job has been serving as part of a cooperatively owned biofuel fueling station called Biofuel Oasis, in Berkeley. In the spring of 2009, they opened a brand spanking new "green station," with easy access to the freeway (on Ashby and Sacramento). The conversion from an old fueling station with the words "Candy Man Car Wash" out front has changed into one of the greenest fueling stations in the country—and now it has an urban farming store to boot. Bee supplies, livestock feed, and a library of information provide the community all they need to know about urban homesteading. During the day, Novella slings reclaimed veggie diesel and by night is back tending her goats, chickens, and other animals at Ghost Town Farm.

As ruthless as this Queen-of-Hearts approach may sound (that tom was on his way to hanger anyway since it was close to Thanksgiving), Novella feels that if we really want to live closer to our food, we're all going to have to deal with it—noise, smell, and more noise are all part and parcel of working farms. For some, it's a little too much. But just imagine what our country would be like if growing food and/or raising small animals were a prerequisite to graduating from high school. Children would be connected to the joy, sweat, and understanding in what goes into making a meal and bringing food to the table. For some kids, 4-H and FFA provide this experience, but those organizations still only encompass a small percentage of the millions of kids living in the United States, most of whom are completely disconnected from their food. Inevitably this is expressed when they are adults, too.

In addition to her own, Novella estimates that there are around twenty houses growing animals for food in the Oakland area and is "sure more people are doing it too—they're just not white people that write blogs about it like me," she says with laughter. This is especially true in East Oakland, where she reports that urban populations of Latinos, Asians and others are culturally more accustomed to raising small city livestock for food—primarily chickens, rabbits, and other small animals—than their white counterparts. With the rise of chicken- and goat-keeping in the city, today's urban homesteads are reminiscent of days past when gardens and small flocks provided critical protein and sustenance. As Novella explains, prior to anti-immigration zoning and legislation that sought to ban it in the 1940s and '50s, "There used to be pastured cows on Forty-Second Street in Oakland," she says, "and Fruitvale was, well, orchards." Italians back then imported their food culture, and people would keep rabbits because they were everything a chicken wasn't—quiet and easy. "When most cities banned animal husbandry, what they were really banning was various ethnicities and food cultures," she says.

While Novella acknowledges that there are some credible reasons why cities passed bans, such as the non-permissible practice of keeping cows locked in garages, the all-or-nothing approach is detrimental to realizing the full potential of urban food production. So before

Adventures in Pigs

Perhaps one of Novella's most entertaining endeavors at Ghost Town Farm has been her rendezvous in raising pigs. Calling herself "pork motivated," she recounts raising two pigs entirely by dumpster diving in order quench her pork lust.

"I had read in a book that young pigs needed lots of protein and that Norwegian farmers would feed them fish guts, so Bill and I went to Chinatown in downtown Oakland and opened that sick dumpster and pulled out all the fish guts. We would get home and the pigs would be so excited! They loved it. After that we graduated to more 'high-end dining' and started going to Eccolo for northern Italian cuisine. Sometimes we would get caught in a dumpster. One time at Eccolo, this guy in an Italian suit came out and said, 'What are you doing?' and I said, 'I have pigs.' 'Keep going,' he said."

Novella finally met owner Chris Lee with, "Hey, I have two pigs and I love your dumpster" as an opening line. Chris was really curious as to why someone would possibly want to have pigs in Oakland. Luckily for her, he appreciated her pork motivation, and the meeting provided her with just the connection she needed. After granting her VIP full-access privileges to the dumpsters, Chris agreed to teach her how to make salami in-house. The enormity of the pigs' carcasses and what had to be done to process all of that meat would have been daunting without his help and state-of-the-art kitchen. (Novella's freezer definitely could not have handled two three-hundred-pounders.)

People still ask Novella when she's going to raise another pig. Her answer: not anytime soon. "A three-hundred-pound pig eats *a lot* of food, and there were two of them," she says exasperatedly. She thinks that next time she would raise a pig communally, like some people in London have done in the past. This way everyone could help with feeding the pigs, and everyone would get a share of meat, too.

As Novella dumpster dove all of their food (daily when they were bigger), this made the pigs the lowest carbon-footprinted meat possible. Conventional meat, especially beef, is one of the least environmentally friendly foods, as it relies on water, crops for food, and transportation, and contributes to global warming.

starting your own city flock, be sure to check with your city zoning and codes—each city varies slightly. In Oakland, for example, it's fine to keep chickens and roosters, but in Berkeley, right next door, no roosters are allowed—they're just too noisy! In El Cerrito, a suburb in the Bay just north of Berkeley, some neighbor complained years ago about chicken noise and now the city only allows Bantams, a specific breed that they claim is not nearly as loud, dusty, or annoying as other chickens—an uneducated conclusion.

Beyond being a hub for educating all of us who care to listen, Novella's ongoing experiment at Ghost Town has reaped more rewards than just pork, eggs, and milk. She's pleased to see what has come out of the eclectic yet scrappy community that she belongs to and cares so much about. "We built this squat garden and every day I look down there and see people picking things and I love that. It doesn't have to be an organization; it can be a person. People get caught up in the idea that they have to be a part of something. My advice is to just go for it! There are so many abandoned lots. We need more gumption! I'm hoping my book will inspire people to do stuff." *The Complete Urban Farmer* is a how-to book that Novella and Willow Rosenthal are publishing together and is sure to be well received as the new bible of backyard farming.

Whatever Novella gets into next on Ghost Town Farm, both *Farm City* and *The Complete Urban Farmer* will undoubtedly help people take over abandoned lots, start guerilla gardens, get some chickens, kill some turkeys, and regain a sense of independence from our current industrial food system.

RECIPES FOR ACTION

The farm to city concept didn't used to be so abstract; our food used to come from our city's planned "farm edges." Today gardeners, activists and urban planners alike are working to reincorporate the production of food in, around, and on top of our most densely populated places, our cities. There are numerous ways that you as an eater, farmer, or food business can foster urban food production. Here are some ideas.

EATER

As an eater, you can grow your own, buy from your farmers market, or play a role in supporting urban farming networks.

Here's how you can plug in:

- Start an urban farm in your neighborhood. Take over an abandoned lot. Ideally, get permission first.
- Grow food at your house. If you don't have soil, use pots or find out if there's a community garden near you.
- Buy food from existing urban farm projects and encourage local businesses to do so. As an eater, your opinion and dollars mean a lot to businesses.
- Donate your time or whatever resources you might have to urban farming projects, whether it's digging holes, designing websites, or spreading the gospel of their good work through your social networks.

FARMER

Mentorship and provision of food to urban populations is critical to ensuring that our urban populations stay connected to their food. You can participate by:

- Encouraging farm sites to be developed in urban areas.
- Helping set up a farm stand and provide product for urban farming projects.
- Selling your food at local farmers markets. Work with your market to be able to accept Food Stamps and WIC dollars and consider donating your leftover product to organizations that redistribute to people who need it (food banks, Food Not Bombs, etc.).

FOOD BUSINESS

By creating relationships within your community, you benefit from the positive media that comes out of collaboration. There are numerous ways that businesses can support urban farming efforts:

- Help an urban farm with storage or processing of their farm products in your certified kitchen.
- Host an event to support your local urban farm.
- Buy food from an urban farm.
- Compost your food waste at an urban farm site by providing access to your dumpsters.

CHAPTER 6

THE NEXT GENERATION OF SUSTAINABLE FARMERS

According to the last agricultural census, in the years between 2002 and 2007, 291,329 new farms began operation. That means that hundreds of thousands of farmers out there are "greenhorns"—agricultural rookies. And, while the current average age of a farm operator is fifty-seven, for these new farms the average age is forty-eight.[1] The decreasing age of farmers and increased growth in the number of farms signals a change in the way that people want to live, do business, and interact with the natural world. Even though farming can be daunting, more people are choosing it as a way of life.

One of the Central Valley of California's longstanding organic farmers once said that the United States needs to post a public service announcement calling for new farmers that reads: "Wanted: 30,000,000 New Farmers to Feed America." This is roughly 10 percent of our population and would be a dramatic increase from the last reported number of less than 2 percent of us that are currently engaged in farming.

The barriers to entering farming to many prospective greenhorns can be economic, physical, and meteorological in nature and scope. Unless one possesses a small fortune, the implements needed for success—barns, irrigation, greenhouses, and tractors—cannot be coaxed from the soil. Not to mention the question of what to grow: Which varieties? What will do well on the land? If there's meat involved, who will process it? Where will it be sold? Then there is the physical toll of farming: the job requires getting up early, oftentimes working past dark, and repeating it again the next day, six or seven days a week. And thanks to global climate change and fluctuating temperatures, it's a lot more difficult to predict the weather. These days planting and harvesting schedules get thrown out the window.

Despite these challenges, new farmers are hearing the call to return to the land and are jumping right into a lifestyle that beckons them. Fortunately, farming is still a desirable occupation for all of those hundreds of thousands of new farmers out there. As the

"Greenhorns Handbook" puts it: "American agriculture is in crisis. A crisis of toxicity. A crisis of monoculture. A crisis of control. A crisis of obesity. But also, a crisis of attrition. Industrial agriculture is having a hard time convincing young people to get involved in factory farming. The good news is that ever-increasing numbers of young people are entering sustainable agriculture successfully."[2]

Youth Organizations for Local Food

The show ring is dusty from animals prancing around as judges review their shoulders and shanks. High school students are showing off a year's worth of hard work and demonstrate a menagerie of farm life—pigs of various breeds, cows, goats, rabbits, and others— at their county fair. At the end of the day, the winner gets an added bonus as ribbons earn them higher prices for their auctioned animals. Many of the kids pay for college this way, but also earn invaluable life skills. It is here, at county and state fairs, where the students of Future Farmers of America (FFA) and 4-H—the two longest running associations promoting food and agriculture as life skills to youth— show off their hard work.

This scene could be your own county fair. Still one of the best places to get down with your local community and see what kind of culture around food and agriculture is alive and well: jam tastings, largest pumpkin contests, best berry pie, and other kinds of homegrown goodness presented in tents and fairground buildings. As far as the next generation of farmers goes, the FFA and 4-H are the longest standing organizations engaging youth about these issues. Both have different tracks of agriculture, community service, and oftentimes, animal husbandry.

The 4-H Pledge

"I pledge my Head to clearer thinking, my Heart to greater loyalty, my Hands to larger service, and my Health to better living . . . for my club, my community, my country and my world."

4-H started in 1902 in Ohio as a way to encourage youth to engage in agriculture and as a way to introduce new technology to adults. Researchers at land grant colleges found that when youth shared new ideas with adults, they were more receptive. This is still the case, and in 1914, the USDA created the Cooperative Extension Service, which included boys' and girls' clubs that later became known as 4-H. The goal of 4-H is to bring together "students, teachers and agribusiness to solidify support for agricultural education." (Based on 2007 estimates, 4-H has 6 million students engaged in their activities nationwide.)

Future Farmers of America (FFA) started a little bit later in 1928. FFA estimates that "millions of agriculture students—no one knows exactly how many—have donned the official FFA jacket and championed the FFA creed." Both organizations provide students with leadership skills and career training through agricultural education.

While 4-H and FFA are primarily set up for pre-college students, the growing farm-to-institution momentum has not been lost on students. A new, progressive organization has formed to rise to the challenge of promoting sustainable agriculture and food on university campuses across the United States. *The Real Food Challenge* provides a network and a campaign as "colleges and universities spend over $4 billion each year on food. This figure represents a significant portion of the national food system—one that young people can directly influence." Their website, www .realfoodchallenge.org, has numerous resources on how to work to transition food, including "A Guide to Sustainable Food Purchasing" and other resources for how to work with food service providers. As the Community Alliance with Family Farmers resource on this site points out, food service businesses can even save money if they're smart about how they buy. Solutions to incorporating local foods at no additional cost to an institution include encouraging farmers markets on campuses and offering vegetarian lunch days (meat is expensive).

Across the country, youth are involved, they are engaged, and they are our future! During our country's transition to regional food systems we will find that at times we must lead, and at other times, we must follow.

SEVERINE VON TSCHARNER FLEMING

FILMMAKER, *THE GREENHORNS*

The Greenhorns is a documentary that looks at the lives, drive and passion of young farmers.

FARMER, SMITHEREEN FARM + SPECIAL PRODUCE, HUDSON, NEW YORK

Smithereen Farm is a small diversified meat, vegetable, and flower farm.

Once you meet Severine, you never forget her. The name, the curly hair, the foldable bike, or whatever bike she happens to be riding, all leave an impact. While on tour around the country filming and promoting her documentary, *The Greenhorns,* she simultaneously manages a two-and-one-quarter-acre farm called Smithereen Farm + Special Produce, where she raises meat rabbits, pigs, chickens, ducks, flowers, herbs, and all sorts of weird varieties of vegetables.

Severine's perspective on farming is one of optimism. She views people who start out farming for the first time as drivers for social and environmental change, saying, "The good thing about farming is that it produces a real product, turning sunshine into calories. It's a little bit more resilient than other structures we have." Severine evolved her affinity for rural places and farming as a lifestyle during her childhood summer vacations on her mother's farm in Switzerland. "It affected my life," she says, "the dappled shade, sunlight in the straw. I'm not anti-urban but am against the tendency that people have to look at rural as provincial. I guess I would say I'm anti-skyscraper."

Growing up in Cambridge, Massachusetts, with intellectual urban-planning–activist parents, Severine learned by watching. According to her, before she was even two years old, she had traveled to over forty states with her parents, tagging along on their research trail from her car seat. Her mom co-founded Women's Action for Nuclear Disarmament (WAND) in the 1980s, and her house was always full of conspiratorial women. The kitchen was for meals, but also for board meetings. "I've noticed the same in sustainable agriculture," she says. "Women are talking through all the networking and collaboration. It's non-competitive and non-chauvinistic. Young women take on responsibility and non-glamorous things in ways that boys do not." She knows this through her experience starting a student farm and garden on the campus of Pomona College. While the men involved would take on the infrastructure building, she would write the plans and manage the logistics of signage, institutional interface and other essential tasks—all in service to the project. Severine believes that sustainable agriculture is really benefiting from all the female involvement. She's joined by a cadre of women, in urban and rural places, that are putting the moves on food production in a similar way that her mother did in the 1970s on weapons issues. "We still need some more men, but the women are critical contributors to the very lasting institutions of sustainable food," says Severine.

DOCUMENTING THE LIVES OF YOUNG FARMERS

The Greenhorns is Severine's documentary film about young farmers that has blossomed into a national network. She's very encouraged by all of the progress and the interest in food and farming, saying, "I think there are 10 percent of us that are innately plant people. *The Greenhorns* hopes to awaken the 'farmer inside' for twelve to twenty-two-year-old viewers—and to make farmer-supporters of other viewers." The movie provides inspiring insight into the lives, drive and passion of young people from California to New York.

Many of the new farmers getting into agriculture do not come from farming backgrounds, so Severine is consolidating resources on the Greenhorns website (thegreenhorns.net) and has created a "Greenhorns Handbook" for distribution to those without access to the Internet. She is hopeful that the increase in numbers of newer farms will translate into better government assistance for farms that have been operating for less than ten years—in both the capital and the land departments. She points out that in Ireland, organic farmers get a 50 percent match on their infrastructure investments such as barns, warehouses and processing facilities. We're hardly there, but we're on our way.

In the United States, the 2008 Farm Bill allocated $27 million for the Beginning Farmers and Ranchers Program, a step up from the previous Farm Bill's provisions. But until now, the government has done very little to support small farms. In fact, with suffocating regulations and increasing mandates for on-farm requirements, the legislature at present is financially prohibitive for smaller growers. This new source of funding does provide some assistance along with a few other ways young farmers can access land and facilities. The aging farming population is one such resource; aging farmers wanting to keep their land in production are often interested in working with younger people. Additionally, a new set of landowners interested in partnering with new farmers for personal, philanthropic, or tax-based reasons are coming in and encouraging partnerships. Lastly, in the case of changing government awareness about food and farming, Parks departments are being considered for food production on public spaces in new ways. From "The Greenhorns Handbook": "As a beginning farmer it may seem near impossible to get your hands into soil you can call your own but do not despair, the land is there—its just a matter of the 'step by step' progression towards getting tenured access to it."

SMITHEREEN FARM + SPECIAL PRODUCE

Severine is enjoying the process of filmmaking and of connecting with other greenhorns and their allies from around the country. "I'm getting to meet all these people from Ohio, Florida, and all over, and they all have the same story. They are fierce and they all had naysayers, but they all did it anyway. It gives me a lot of courage. There's a certain amount of ballsiness that goes along with it and you feel driven to make change and initiate like a pioneer. I really cherish that sense of independence."

In New York state's Hudson Valley, Severine's egg-shaped two-and-one-quarter acres hum with diversity. She's learning the ropes by growing a variety of herbs, cut flowers, veggies, four kinds of dried squash, chickens, ducks, and her twenty-seven or so rabbits for meat.

She encourages any new greenhorn thinking about meat production to "start really small with all of your ideas and observe the archetype of the animal that you are interested in raising and read all about them. Go to the feed store, figure it out small and go bigger next year. Grow your operation and your business organically! It sounds obvious, but, as farming is working with living creatures, it's good to limit your casualties."

"There's a certain amount of ballsiness that goes along with farming and you feel driven to make change and initiate like a pioneer."

Speaking of ups and downs, "The average human doesn't have enough contact with natural systems to understand the limitations and resilience of agricultural systems," explains Severine. "Only through experience do we learn the efficacy of our natural world." Her standard, matter-of-fact tone speaks volumes.

As Severine is reclaiming the integrity of farming, her parents have caught the bug too. "My parents are proud that I'm going to be a farmer, and that I'm capturing stories and manufacturing the rhetoric of sustainable agriculture." This is just the opposite reaction that many people receive when they tell their families that they are going to work the land. Long hailed as grueling labor, land-based work is being reclaimed as work that carries the utmost integrity. Unexpectedly, these hard economic times have opened some ears. She's finding that the "losing-all-of-your-money thing has been a real boon in these conversations."

Severine's exuberance and assertion that another world is possible is a welcome message today. "Let's have a strategic subsidy that values sustainability!" she says. "Let us be proactive, prescriptive, working on behalf of the populace instead!" It's a message that screams with heart and verve that yes, you too can take your future into your own hands, and even start farming someday.

ZOË BRADBURY

FARMER, VALLEY FLORA FARM, LANGLOIS, OREGON

Valley Flora Farm is a small family farm that provides fresh local food to CSA customers and local restaurants.

WRITER, *EDIBLE PORTLAND* AND *DIARY OF A YOUNG FARMER*

Zoë Bradbury, the youngest of a mom and two-daughter farming trio, is plopping the last of the season's tomato harvest into canning jars. It's a good time to think about what to grow next year and assess the successes and defeats of the various crops she planted—artichokes, strawberries, and various annual vegetables that the local community gobbled up enthusiastically. In this rich agricultural area on the southern Oregon coast, just a few crops dominate the landscape: cranberries, sheep, cattle, and hay, most of which, Zoë points out, are not eaten locally. Not even the local seafood is eaten here. Ironically, the fish and chips joint serves battered Alaskan cod even though it is located one hundred yards from the dock where local fishermen are hauling live rockfish, tuna, and cod out of the hold for export to the Bay Area.

Perhaps this is why the neighbors of Valley Flora are eating whatever the farm can grow with gusto. Betsy, Abby, and Zoë are the only produce operation in town. Their small family farm began with a homespun salad greens business that Abby started twelve years ago. Now, the three of them collectively grow upwards of one hundred fresh market crops that they pool for their growing CSA and restaurant markets, all within a fifty-mile radius.

Valley Flora is as pretty it sounds, nestled in an idyllic river valley tucked into the coast range four miles from the Pacific Ocean. The farm is composed of forty acres of flat, fertile bottomland, hillside pasture and woods, cut through by Floras Creek. It's a special microclimate on this stretch of the Oregon coast, where just two miles further west, the fog rolls in thick and cold in the summer.

For Zoë, when she headed off into the world, she never really left the land that her mom, Betsy, settled down on thirty-five years ago.

"Growing up here, being born on this land . . . this place is in my blood. It has always been the core of my universe."

Leaving the farm after high school to travel and pursue her undergraduate work, Zoë ended up at Stanford University in California. She graduated with a degree in Ecological Anthropology in 2001, and then headed off to work for some of California's most notable food and farming non-profits. These included San Francisco's Center for Urban Education of Sustainable Agriculture (CUESA) that runs the famous Ferry Plaza Farmers Market, and the Agriculture and Land Based Training Association (ALBA) in the Salinas Valley—the salad bowl of the nation—where she worked with an immigrant farmer training program.

After a few years, her homing instinct propelled her north again to her native Oregon.

The food scene in Portland, Oregon, is alive and booming with vibrant farmers markets, local food restaurants, hipster retail co-ops, and even a university that features local farmers' foods. This is where Zoë moved in 2003 to take up a job as Crew Leader at Sauvie Island Organics. Located just fifteen miles from downtown, the farm has been a stalwart of organic food production since 1993. It was here that Zoë learned the ropes of growing food for their two hundred CSA members and over twenty-five Portland restaurant accounts on sixteen acres of the farm's beautifully loamy soil.

After three years of farming at Sauvie Island Organics, Zoë knew that grad school loomed on the horizon. She was looking at two options for graduate work—a full-ride fellowship in rural sociology at Cornell University or an independent Masters program through Antioch. As she was already scheming about her eventual move back to Floras Creek, she opted for the Antioch program.

Over those two years of grad school working towards her Masters in Community Change and Civic Leadership with a focus on food systems, she also worked for Eco Trust, a leading nonprofit working on sustainable agriculture and environmental issues in Portland.

Her studies and time in Portland would lay the groundwork for realizing her life dream: to return to Floras Creek and farm for herself on the family land. "I always knew I would eventually trade the city for the swimming hole," she laughs. "It was only a matter of time."

Planning for farming takes time and money. So Zoë enrolled in an Individual Development Account (IDA) program to start saving seed money for the business. She got busy crunching numbers, working on crop plans, and sculpting her marketing plan. By the time she moved back to Langlois, she had her fields mapped out and was wrapping up her masters. "When I started farming in spring of 2007," says Zoë, "I had one more class and an honors thesis to go. It was a stretch, but I managed to get it done—pushing through the first six months of farming while finishing my graduate program."

THE WRITING FARMER

Zoë didn't set about just to cultivate vegetables, though. Since grade school, she has also loved to write and has brought her dual passion for the pitchfork and the pen together as she's taken the leap into farming over the past few years. She writes regularly for *Edible Portland,* pens a weekly CSA newsletter, writes monthly essays for *Diary of a Young Farmer,* and in the winter publishes work in various other print and online outlets.

Zoë jokes in one of her online blog posts that if she were smarter, she would have started having children in high school because by this time, they would be teenagers and able to help out on the farm. In one post, she writes about how challenging and physically exhausting it can be managing the fields: "I have been swallowed by September—enveloped in the folds of peak harvest. The heirloom tomatoes are on. The cabbage is ripe and huge and gorgeous. The leeks are fat. The corn is ready. The sunflowers are nodding under the weight of their own seed." Two kids in their early teens certainly would have remedied the harvest situation.

The fact that Zoë writes on the side is a unique twist: "I've always loved to write, but during my junior year at Stanford, I decided against an English major and pursued ecology and anthropology. For some reason, I carried this myth that writers don't change the world, that they aren't 'activist.' But little by little, I began to recognize the difference writers can make—Michael Pollan's *Omnivore's Dilemma* was a great example." In 2007 she was awarded a Food and Society Policy Fellowship—a prestigious two-year fellowship that goes to a handful of writers, filmmakers, educators, activists—and, yes, even farmers—who are working to promote a healthy, green, and fair food system. Zoë has used her fellowship to write about the issues facing beginning farmers in the United States today, and to rally support for the next generation of sustainable farmers—a critical cause at a time when the average age of American farmers is fifty-seven, and over a quarter of all farmers are sixty-five or older.[3]

THE WOMEN OF VALLEY FLORA FARM

Zoë gives a lot of the credit for starting the business in the first place to growing up on her mom's farm and to her sister. Zoë grew up in the old red and white farmhouse that her mom, Betsy, still lives in today. "My mom didn't make money the top priority but recognized the value of this life. She's the kind of person who can wield a chain saw and knitting needles with equal grace," says Zoë, describing Betsy as the "Jill of all trades."

Betsy's garden was vast and the pantry and freezer were always brim-full with homegrown food. But it wasn't until 1997 that the farm shifted towards commercial production, selling to their neighbors and local businesses. In high school, Abby and Zoë decided to experiment with their own business venture: a pesto farm. Together, they planted garlic at Christmas break, but it proved to be a bad year to start production farming. The El Niño winter, with record floods and winds, drowned out their garlic crop in the bottomland of their property under the waves of floodwaters. Come spring, it was clear that the garlic crop was a near-loss, and without the garlic, they couldn't imagine the pesto business coming to fruition.

So they did what any farmer does—shifted gears.

Abby decided to plant salad greens—Thai Green, Red Sails, Merlot, Redina, Emerald Oak, Reine Des Glaces, twenty-six different varieties of direct-seeded lettuces, Asian greens, edible flowers, and specialty Mesclun Mix—for sale to local restaurants. "There was a lot of skepticism at first," recounts Zoë. "No one was growing produce in our area, and very few farms were direct marketing. My sister was quite the pioneer here." Season after season, Abby built a loyal following of buyers who appreciated the quality, beauty, freshness and flavor of "Abby's Greens."

Abby did this all while finishing her undergraduate degree, so every fall when she would pack up and head to the East Coast, Betsy would take over. Betsy invested in a couple of greenhouses to keep the salad production going through the winter and then used the greenhouses for summer production of tomatoes, peppers, cucumbers, basil and other hot weather crops that don't ripen readily outdoors on the Oregon coast. Together, this mother-daughter duo paved the way for Zoë's return in 2007, when she moved back to Langlois to team up with them to help start Valley Flora.

The threesome operates in a unique way, each running her own business and taking charge of her own crops, but marketing all of their produce collectively.

Abby is the "Greens Queen," overseeing all of the summer salad production; Betsy focuses on greenhouse production of summer crops and winter salad mix; and Zoë grows a wide array of outdoor row crops, perennials, and berries. "All together, we're growing and marketing upwards of a hundred different crops on the farm. It's a dance— one that we all have to work hard to choreograph together."

One of the keys to their success farming as a family is the fact that everyone is her own boss. "It's important to all of us that we have a certain level of independence, autonomy and creative freedom," says Zoë, who started the CSA portion of their business. They all bring their products together twice a week for their CSA and restaurant deliveries, something that Zoë takes great joy in. "I love packing out the shares each week and seeing the beauty of the produce we grow. There's a maxim around here, coined by my mom, that everything we do has to be at least 51 percent art."

Today the Valley Flora CSA is up to fifty-five members and they have a waiting list longer than

"There's a maxim around here that everything we do has to be at least 51 percent art."

the number of subscribers. Zoë points out, "It's not Portland or San Francisco. It's a rural, conservative, working class, in a remote part of Oregon—but people here are just as hungry for local food." Like other agricultural parts of the country the majority of food produced in Curry County—lamb, cattle, cranberries, fish—is mostly for export. "There's such abundance here, and more and more people are interested in tapping into local sources for produce and protein. It gives me hope for other places in the country that aren't the Portlands and the San Franciscos of the world." Zoë notes that most farmers orient to the larger cities to market their goods, but that the women at Valley Flora don't feel disadvantaged to be three hours from the nearest metropolis. Quite the opposite.

"Every week I get to have these great interactions with our CSA members—someone who is newly enamored with hakurei turnips, or thrilled about the strawberries—and that connection makes all the hard work worth it," says Zoë.

THE CHALLENGES OF STARTING A FARM

Getting to this point hasn't been easy, though. Zoë still has the taste of her first spring lingering in her memory. It's early 2008 and "spring," she says, "has been a really wild ride." Even though she'd saved money for her startup, there was no avoiding the cash flow crisis that plagued her first few months in business.

Starting up a farm isn't cheap, and although Zoë was fortunate to have family land to return to, nevertheless she had to make major investments in infrastructure to get her business off the ground: a propagation greenhouse, an irrigation system, a mile of deer fencing, a barn, a walk-in cooler, a delivery van, and an expensive new power service. She needed tools and equipment, harvest supplies and seed, soil amendments and marketing materials. The list was long and pricey. She estimates that startup costs in her first two years totaled more than $50,000.

Zoë did everything she could to make use of available financial resources during those two years: the IDA program helped her afford a barn on the property, and her savings bought her a greenhouse and some essential farm equipment. But it wasn't enough. In March of 2008, she went to the USDA Farm Service Agency (FSA) hoping to qualify for their Beginning Farmer Loan Program, but soon learned that she was ineligible for the funds she needed to pay for her buried irrigation mainline because she was technically farming on rented land.

Even had she been able to qualify for a loan, it would have been a meager sum. The loan amount, explained the FSA agent, would be based on her total projected income assessed on current commodity prices for what she was growing. Because Zoë was direct marketing all of her crops, she was getting a far higher price than the commodity list: $2/lb. for carrots instead of $0.15/lb.; $4/lb. for asparagus, not $0.45/lb.; $1/lb. for winter squash, not $0.06/lb. At those prices, she would have been lucky to qualify for $5,000 through FSA.

Desperate at this point for the funds she needed, she started shopping around for 0 percent credit cards—a short-term solution to cover her mounting startup debt, and one that left her nervous. The 0 percent card bought her some time, but whether it would be enough time was unclear. Sadly, it was the only option as there weren't any government funding resources out there for young farmers like her wanting to farm sustainably.

In addition to the financial stresses, there's Mother Nature to deal with: the good seasons and the bad, the storms and the sunshine. Life doesn't stop bringing surprises when you make your living from the land, surprises that sometimes can be catastrophic. On Zoë's stretch of the Oregon coast, winter brings one-hundred-mile-per-hour winds (flat crops) and heavy floods (root rot). There are late freezes (busted pipes) and summer onslaughts of cucumber beetles (no food). The potential list of natural and infrastructural disasters is pretty lengthy and this is why some farmers have crop insurance, although, as Zoë points out, it usually doesn't apply to farms like hers.

"The thing about crop insurance is that it's not well designed for diversified farmers like us. Growing a monocrop of corn or soy is one thing, but when you have one hundred different crops—a bed of this, an $^1/_8$ of an acre of that—it's tough," says Zoë. "I don't buy crop insurance; my crop insurance is diversity and to a certain extent, CSA. By trying to farm in the most holistic and ecological way I can, I'm trying to build in some natural defenses from pests, inclement weather, and all the other unforeseens."

It's not always enough, though. Zoë recounts how devastating it was when a freak hailstorm tore through in early June last year. "It was the second week of June, right when everything was succulent and tender—just sizing up and setting fruit. Some farmers saw their entire farm devastated in a matter of minutes: heads of lettuce shredded, melons punctured with holes; peaches riddled with pockmarks; tomato blossoms torn from the plants. "It's unbelievable the kind of loss that is possible, when you're at that point in the season, on the cusp of harvest. We fortunately were spared." In response to the storm, farmers helped each other out by offering new plant starts to those hardest hit, but many were set back by months.

All of these challenges aside, "There's not a day that goes by that I don't look up and feel happy to be here on this land, home. It's a beautiful place, a community that I love, and I'm grateful to be able to live a lifestyle that is also a livelihood," she says. For Zoë, farming is the most meaningful existence she can possibly imagine. "No day is the same. Farming is challenging in so many ways, physically and mentally. To be a good diversified farmer you have to be a systems thinker and that's something that doesn't come easy. Farming is one part intellect, one part intuition, one part muscle, and one part heart. And beyond that, it's mostly out of my control."

STRIKING THE WORK/LIFE BALANCE

Zoë's passion for sustainable agriculture reaches beyond production practices alone. "Farming also has to be sustainable for me personally, which means having time for family, not always working until dark, not beating my body up or feeling perennially stressed about money. It's hard to achieve that when you're growing produce and life is driven by the tilt of the earth and photosynthesis. But I've learned to ask myself: How do I want this one life to look and feel?"

A few things are for sure: that there be time for a dip at the swimming hole on hot summer days, that she have the space to pause and appreciate the swallows dipping and diving over the field, or the time to savor June's first raspberries. "Abby and I both have ivy-league degrees and I can't count the number of times people have wondered why we chose to be farmers instead of doctors or lawyers or bankers. The answer is partly in all of those little things that we love about each day, the things that go unaccounted for: good food in abundance, the autonomy of self-employment and the beauty. None of these things are part of the bottom line in Quickbooks, but they're the things that make this life so rich."

And ultimately, hopes Zoë, our culture will once again look upon farmers with the same respect that doctors garner today. "It's pretty simple," she sums. "No farmers, no food. I'm proud to be one of the next generation of farmers this country needs. Now for recruiting the next 50 million . . ."

RECIPES FOR ACTION

Young farmers, especially those that don't come to farming through their families, need our support in a different way than farms that have existed for longer periods of time. Here are ways that we can help support the next crop of farmers, so that they too can carry on the traditions of farming and producing food for us and future generations.

EATER

As an eater, here are some ways that you can help young farmers:

- Try to identify new farms at your farmers market and make a point of buying their foods.
- Search for new farms online at eatwellguide.org or localharvest.org.
- If you're able to find new farmers, see if you can volunteer for them. A skilled volunteer, especially in web or graphic design, can provide the necessary tools they may need to succeed.
- Find out what markets they are interested in expanding to (CSA, restaurant, retail, etc.). Request their products and do outreach on their behalf.

FARMER

You can encourage the next generation by:

- Inviting a young farmer over for lunch.
- Joining Farm Link, a national organization that promotes farmer-to-farmer exchanges.
- Taking opportunities to speak at a local school. You never know what seeds will be planted for youngsters.
- Considering implementing an intern, WWOOF (Willing Workers Of Organic Farms), or other learning exchange or apprentice program on your farm. While it will require work on your end, the learning exchange will prove to be invaluable to you and the young farmers that you share your knowledge with.

FOOD BUSINESS

Your business can ensure the success of young farmers. For example, restaurateur Jesse Cool buys "whatever farmers can grow." Consider partnering with a young farmer and supporting them by:

- Educating your customers about them.
- Helping young farmers reach other businesses.
- Hosting a community event in celebration of the young farmers, their food, and the seasons.

SUSTAINABLE AGRICULTURE FOR A SUSTAINABLE CLIMATE

By Renata Brillinger, director of Californians for GE-Free Agriculture and co-founder of the California Climate and Agriculture Network

Farming holds the key to our future, not only in the food that we grow and raise but also in combating the number one environmental and economic challenge of our time—global climate change.

Climate change touches all aspects of human activity, including our sources of energy and how we transport people and goods, build our infrastructure, and feed and clothe ourselves. Scientists are warning that its effects will be far more significant and sooner than what was predicted just a few years ago.

Bold and innovative leadership is needed in all sectors of society, in every industry, and at every scale. We must re-imagine our energy and transportation infrastructure, land use patterns, and economic priorities if we are to avert the worst impacts of climate change on earth's ecosystems and on future human generations.

Agriculture and food systems are no exception. In fact, agriculture is arguably the human practice most vulnerable to the environmental chaos of climate change, and one of the most essential ingredients of our daily activities. If ever there was a time for a rigorous, analytical, demonstrable and replicable sustainable agriculture system to be described, funded and implemented, that time is now.

Agriculture is responsible globally for approximately 15 percent of all greenhouse gas (GHG) emissions.[1] Two of the most potent greenhouse gases—methane and nitrous oxide—are produced almost entirely by agricultural activity. Almost all of the world's nitrous oxide emissions come from fertilizer applications (which is 298 times more potent than CO_2); two-thirds of all methane emissions (twenty-five times more potent than CO_2) come from agriculture. In addition, one-third of all CO_2 emissions come from forest clearing for agricultural purposes in developing countries.[2]

As we have seen before with the problem of world hunger, the biotechnology industry is using the problem of climate change to advance its agenda, promising that it can genetically engineer biofuels and climate-adapted crops with high-tech, privately controlled and patented, genetically engineered crops and synthetic microorganisms. There is no evidence that they will be any more successful with this approach than they have been in solving world hunger, which remains a problem of food distribution and access, not a problem of global food scarcity. Genetic engineering has been unsuccessful in increasing crop yields,[3] and scientists are finding it very difficult if not impossible to use genetic engineering techniques to develop complex, multi-gene traits such as drought and heat tolerance.

On the other hand, sustainable agriculture offers an array of natural solutions to address these growing concerns with the capacity to reduce GHG emissions, sequester carbon, produce on-farm renewable energy and fertilizer, and also prepare farmers to adapt their crops and soil for climate change.

The following sustainable solutions could be greatly enhanced with just a fraction of the research and marketing dollars that are currently being devoted to industrial agriculture and genetic engineering.

(1) Increase Biodiversity

A 2008 United Nations Food and Agriculture Organization (FAO) report concludes that "as climate changes, the value of biodiversity for food and agriculture will increase. Genetic resources are the living material that local communities, researchers and breeders use to adapt food and agricultural production to changing needs. Maintaining and using this reservoir of genetic diversity inherent knowledge of our Native peoples and indigenous cultures around the world, will be the foundation for coping with climate change."[4]

Right now, genetic engineering and patenting of traditional seed varieties by private corporations presents a threat to agricultural diversity.

(2) Reduce GHG Emissions

Agriculture emits three greenhouse gases—carbon dioxide from burning fossil fuels, nitrous oxide primarily from synthetic fertilizer applications, and methane from animal waste. Just as in every industry, agriculture is challenged to find ways to decrease its GHG emissions. The following offer a few solutions:

Decrease Fertilizer and Pesticide Use—Sustainable farming practices use lower rates per acre of fossil fuel inputs than conventional systems, as low as 48 to 66 percent, according to one FAO study.[5]

Improve Energy and Water Efficiency—Because water-related electricity use represents over 90 percent of all electricity used in agriculture,[6] and with pending drought, farmers will need to transition to improved water use efficiency and conservation to reduce both fuel costs of pumping and to save water resources that will be increasingly costly and decreasingly available.

Foster Local Food Movement—Reducing food miles traveled can address GHG emissions in the transportation sector, particularly when the food is grown organically or sustainably. The local food movement is well positioned to help get more local food to market while educating about the relationship between agriculture and climate protection.

Protect Farmland—Creating food belts around urban areas provides a barrier to urban sprawl and facilitates local food systems. Protecting farmland and open space provides opportunities to sequester carbon and protect biodiversity—intelligent farmland protection should preserve the healthiest soils for food production rather than urban growth.

(3) Sequester Carbon

Organic agriculture has great potential for carbon sequestration—the best low-tech and relatively inexpensive solution that pulls carbon out of the air and stores it in the ground. The regular addition of organic matter to soils is the only way to maintain or increase soil organic carbon.[7] Farming could be integrating more carbon-sequestering forests, native grasses and perennial crops

of all kinds to contribute to climate protection, protect riparian zones, and provide wildlife habitat. Existing federal conservation programs should be enhanced to reward farmers integrating climate protection practices, and funding to incentivize farmers to shift to soil sequestration techniques should be increased.

(4) On-Farm Renewable Energy Production

All human activities in a sustainable future must be powered using renewable sources of energy rather than depending on finite and insecure fossil fuels.

Farms that have relatively large land holdings and large energy demands have the potential to produce and use renewable energy from a variety of sources including wind power, solar thermal water heating, and biodigesters to convert manure and plant material to electricity.

These four ready-to-go solutions provided by sustainable agriculture have the potential to combat one of the greatest issues of our time—global climate change—while increasing the abundance, vitality and sustainability of our food and rural communities. As with all truly sustainable approaches, addressing the role of agriculture in climate change will inevitably make a contribution to a sustainable economic future as well.

THE LOWDOWN ON FARM BILL ADVOCACY

By Aimee Witteman, executive director of the National Sustainable Agriculture Coalition

W hat constitutes a position in advocacy is not only limited to working for a nonprofit. It's important to think about all of the other entry points into working on food. There are lots of ways to be an advocate."—Margaret Krome, director of policy, Michael Fields Institute

For decades, federal farm policy has been the intellectual amusement park of none but a few policy wonks and agribusiness lobbyists. The grassroots campaign around the 2008 Farm Bill—with its call for a shift in government subsidies from those that encourage mono-cropped corn and soybeans to programs that promote organic and sustainable agricultural methods—demonstrated that the political landscape around food and farm policy is changing. Average citizens are not only taking notice of what they eat and how their food is grown, but also the role played by government in influencing the choices of farmers and eaters.

In the case of the 2008 Farm Bill, grassroots advocates' efforts paid off. We certainly have a long way to go, but sustained grass-roots pressure on members of the Agriculture Committee during the 2008 Farm Bill resulted in more federal support for organic production, conservation, beginning and minority farmers, and regional food systems than ever before.

Now that we have another five-year interval before the next Farm Bill and other legislative battles to wage around child nutrition, agriculture and climate change, and food safety, the question is not whether our Farm Bill spoils were enough, but how our hard-fought wins can change the food system on the ground and build the movement for long-term policy change. As Rebecca Solnit puts it, "The world is always being made and never finished." In other words, advocating for a better food system is a lifelong endeavor—one Farm Bill fight is not enough.

As we settle in for the long haul, what are the tools and tactics we can use to advance the change we want to see on the farm and in the market?

The advent of "netroots" (online) organizing and public debate in the blogosphere certainly provides advocates new tools to put pressure on members of Congress and on the Department of Agriculture, but some of the best grassroots organizing tactics are still the most basic and low tech.

One of the best things that you can do as a farming and good food advocate is to visit your representative or senators when they are back in the state or district. Check their websites for information about listening sessions or town hall meetings, which they generally conduct when Congress is on recess. Organizing a group visit for farmers and food advocates is even better than going alone. Individuals are important, but individuals working together in groups are powerful agents for social change. If you haven't done so already, find a state-based organization that works on sustainable agriculture and food issues and become a member. If the organization does not already organize visits with members of Congress, volunteer to help them do so.

If you cannot meet with members of Congress face-to-face, fax them a letter or make a phone call to their offices. Individual phone calls and letters to your representatives take just a few minutes of your time, but they collectively add up to a very strong influence on Congressional priorities. The voice of people passionate about family farming and good food needs to be heard in Washington, D.C.

The Capitol Switchboard, (202) 223-3121, can connect you with your senator's or representative's office. In any communication with a member of Congress and his or her office, it is very important that you be as specific as possible. That means naming a specific piece of legislation, program, and funding amount. Again, this is where grassroots member organizations in your state can help. Few of us can be full-time policy advocates and that's where state-based and national advocacy organizations can give you a leg up by providing you an action alert to respond to with specific "asks" of legislators.

Do not forget the power of media! During the latest Farm Bill, the debate over the Agriculture Committee's use of taxpayer dollars was waged in letters to the editor, op-eds, and commentaries penned by sustainable food and agriculture advocates (and certain Berkeley luminaries) in the San Francisco Chronicle and New York Times, as well as regional and farmer-oriented news sources such as the Argus Leader and Iowa Farmer Today. There are a number of excellent food and farming blogs that are also rich sources of information and debate. If you haven't already, check out the Ethicurean.com, Grist.org, and CivilEats.com.

While tenaciously advocating for policies that we want to win, we must also identify what we are against. The policies peddled by powerful agribusiness interests are disguised attempts to increase their international market competitiveness. These policies walk a path that's been unaltered despite a domestic obesity epidemic, persistent food insecurity in our rural and urban communities, a steadily warming planet, and a consumer base clamoring for organic and local foods. Know the enemy, their platform, and their arguments.

A heightened understanding of the relevance of food production to the environment, public health, and social justice is lifting farm and food policy's prominence as a grassroots advocacy tool for leveraging power. The urgency of our current circumstances demands action from each of us. We can make a difference by: 1) acknowledging the essential role that the federal government has in ensuring a healthy and just food system and 2) detailing the ways in which public money can promote the public good through programs that support local and regional markets, the next generation of family farmers, healthy soils, clean water, and sustainably produced foods that are nutritious and accessible to all people. Make your calls for action specific in your visits with legislators, on your phone calls and faxes to their offices, and in the media.

Remember all of these opportunities to tell your story to your representatives. We all eat. We all have a story that is relevant to federal farm and food policy issues.

To stay informed on what is happening on Capitol Hill, and to know when to take action on the issues you care about, please visit the website of the National Sustainable Agriculture Coalition's, www.sustainableagriculture.net, and sign up for our e-newsletter and action alerts.

URBAN AND PERI-URBAN AGRICULTURAL PARKS
By Temra Costa

"Peri," short for "periphery," is land that buffers our urban areas from rural areas and vice versa. These green belts can and should be used to provide fresh fruits and vegetables for the urban residents. Why? Because we can lower the fossil footprint of the agriculture industry and ensure that our cities are better fed.

"Approximately twelve thousand publicly owned lots sit vacant in New York City, enough land to provide jobs and produce food for thousands of people," writes Michael Ableman in *Fatal Harvest*.

In every urban place, there are thousands of such lots—lots that could provide jobs, skill training, and nutritious foods for our urban communities. From the West to the East, cities are re-envisioning their food supply as a matter of food security and are starting to think strategically about urban food production. One exceptional and encouraging change is the number of nationally registered parks that have started to encourage food production on their sites. These lands, perpetually protected from development through their "park zoning" and classification, provide an incredible opportunity to grow food with governmental infrastructure.

Some are calling these areas "agricultural parks," a new twist on publicly funded spaces that promote food production. According to Sustainable Agriculture Education (SAGE) in Berkeley, California, "At an AgPark, nature trails, food production, and agricultural learning—all address economic, health-related, educational, and recreational needs—create multifunctional places that link urban residents and farmers for their mutual benefit." The organization administers the **Sunol Agricultural Park,** a seventeen-acre farm just thirty minutes from Oakland. Here the group fosters potential in new farmers by providing them with parkland that has proximity to

markets in the densely populated Bay Area.

Sibella Kraus, SAGE's president and founder, has been immersed in the Bay Area food realm for more than twenty-five years, working to integrate rural and urban areas. Her innovative approach to encouraging agricultural production within our urban parks systems has promoted greater utilization of this land within urban areas and around the edges that provide a buffer for our invaluable open space and rural areas.

Publicly owned and operated lands are often irrigated and maintained, which can provide essential infrastructure for the production of food. How many times have you seen someone mowing and weeding grassy medians that are never used? Try putting on your food production goggles and see a garden in every vacant publicly owned piece of land. Why not grow food on them? Why couldn't we foster small farm micro-enterprises and bridge the connection between urban and rural?

A few parks departments around the country are truly progressive in that regard. **Queens County Farm Museum** in New York is a great example. Just seven miles from midtown Manhattan, this forty-seven-acre farm may not be enough to feed the nineteen million New York metropolitan residents, but its newly reestablished food production is a start. As the longest continuously farmed parcel in the state, the farm has been owned and operated by the New York City Parks Department since 1975. This plays a large role in why it has not been developed, despite the changes of hand that the property has experienced during its recorded ownership starting in 1697. The Parks Department maintenance has been the primary reason that the farm's agrarian roots have been preserved since it was last farmed in 1926. Offering a range of farm activities such as petting goats, chasing chickens, and milking cows, the farm had been operating under "museum" status for residents of New York that want to experience a farm environment. But as of spring of 2007, the farm is changing.

Kennon Kay, a young farmer living in Brooklyn, was brought on by the farm's director, Michael Robertson, to build upon the farm's first year of success growing vegetables. Destined for their farm stand and the Green Market in Union Square, Kennon and her cadre of interns have a goal of growing the farm's fresh offerings to larger acreages each year.

This is also happening in Chicago at the historic **Wagner Farm.** These "agricultural parks" are able to immediately make sales from good local food due to the large number of visitors that already come to the farms for a farm experience and special events.

Another growing opportunity for urban residents to gain access to local food within their city, in lieu of a historic farm, are **community gardens,** which are typically organized by one person or a group of individuals that create an environment for food production on small sites. If you don't have a backyard, if your soil is marginal, or if your roof can't handle potted plants, a community garden plot might be perfect for you. The American Community Garden Association helps groups get established around the country and provides new gardens with various resources. If there isn't a garden near you, you can search for a local Master Gardener's office—they will be able to find one for you. To find a Master Gardener's office, visit the American Horticultural Society website at: http://www.ahs.org/master_gardeners.

Growing food for your own consumption is the ultimate connection anyone can have with their food. It's rewarding. It's challenging. It's delicious. The benefits will be unimaginable as you create a new way of living in the world and eating with the seasons.

ACKNOWLEDGMENTS

This book wouldn't have been possible without the women featured in these pages. They took time out of their hectic farming, writing, cooking and advocacy lives to add content and robustness.

Thank you to Gibbs Smith, for being the vision behind the book, and Lisa Anderson, my editor, for working her magic; Severine von Tscharner Fleming, for making the connections we need in this world; Logan Rockefeller Harris, an inspiring food activist and the research engine behind this book; and Caiti Hachmyer, who compiled the list of women's agricultural organizations.

Lindsay Dailey, Jennifer Dalton, Jeremy Fisher, Leslie Jackson, Katy Mamen, Caron Obstfeld, Kristen Schroer, Jennifer Snyder, Elanor Starmer, Lisa Thompson, and Taber Ward encouraged, reviewed, and commented to help turn goose liver into foie gras.

Thank you to my parents, Jay and Dianne Costa; my brother, Brett, and his family; my grandparents, Jim and Denise, Selvina and Hank; and my ancestors. Speaking of families, I can't thank Patrick and Sienna Fisher enough for their friendship and for gifting me with such a fabulous human being as their son, Jeremy. He provided me with endless support, encouragement and words of wisdom that kept me going on the project every day (especially the rough ones). A million and one thanks to Lindsay Dailey, who was there to lend a hand, an ear, a meal, and an editing tip until the eleventh hour. Thank you to Melinda Kramer, Leah Katz Ahmadi, and Destin Joy Layne, who were a well of support throughout the process; and Charles Braquet, a saint, for letting me finish editing in his Paris apartment. And where would any of us be without trailblazers and mentors such as Denise O'Brien? She was an advisor to the book and is a pioneer in sustainable agriculture advocacy.

The following were interviewed and/or provided critical insight: Carrie Balkcom, The American Grassfed Beef Association; Brock Dolman, Occidental Arts and Ecology Center; Dana Jackson, The Land Stewardship Project; Kennon Kay, Queens County Farm Museum; Kristen Kordet, Three Moon Farms; Margaret Krome, Michael Fields Institute; Gail Myers, Grow Farms; Karen Parker, Growing Power; and Dorothy Suput, The Carrot Project.

I wouldn't be where I am today without the Community Alliance with Family Farmers, Bioneers, Ecological Farming Association, and the Women's Earth Alliance, all great organizations that have provided me with life changing opportunities and inspiration.

ENDNOTES

INTRODUCTION

1. USDA, 2007 Census of Agriculture.
2. Costa and Rockefeller Harris, "Non-Profit Organizations Gender Demographics."
3. Trendsight, *Marketing to Women* (accessed June 29, 2009).
4. USDA, 2007 Census of Agriculture.

CHAPTER 1

1. The Agriculture Justice Project (accessed May 5, 2009).
2. Hardesty, *Yolo County Producers Lead the Nation in Direct Marketing*, 2005.
3. USDA, 2007 Census of Agriculture.
4. Food and Agriculture Organization of the United Nations, Report on Organics. "Energy Use in Organic Food Systems" (accessed May 5, 2009).
5. Demeter International, "Definition of Biodynamic Agriculture" (accessed May 5, 2009).

CHAPTER 2

1. Cummings, *Uncertain Peril*.
2. Ibid.
3. Food and Agriculture Organization of the United Nations. "The State of Food Insecurity in the World" (accessed June 29, 2009).
4. Food and Agriculture Organization of the United Nations. "Food Price Indices" (accessed June 29, 2009).
5. *The Rush to Ethanol: Not All Biofuels Are Created Equal*. Food and Water Watch, 2007 (accessed June 29, 2009).
6. Lappé and Lappé, *Hope's Edge*.
7. Cummings, *Uncertain Peril*.
8. Martineau, *First Fruit*.
9. Weise, "Americans are iffy on genetically modified foods."
10. Farm to School, http://www.farmtoschool.org/aboutus.php (accessed June 29, 2009).
11. Keeley, "Case Study: Appleton Central Alternative High School's Nutrition and Wellness Program."
12. Nestle, *Food Politics*.
13. Ibid.
14. Farm to School, http://www.farmtoschool.org/aboutus.php (accessed May 5, 2009).

CHAPTER 3

1. Food and Agriculture Organization of the United Nations, "A Matter of Survival" (accessed June 29, 2009).
2. Nabhan, *Renewing America's Food Traditions*.
3. USDA, 2007 Census of Agriculture.

CHAPTER 4

1. Slow Food USA, "Bourbon Red Turkey" (accessed June 29, 2009).
2. USDA, 2002 and 2007, Census of Agriculture.
3. Ibid.
4. United Nations Development Fund for Women (accessed June 29, 2009).
5. Straus Family Creamery, "Frequently Asked Questions: Farm Practices" (accessed June 29, 2009).
6. US Department of Labor. "The National Agricultural Workers Survey 2001–2002" (accessed June 29, 2009).
7. Call, Wendy. "Reclaiming Corn and Culture." *Yes!* Magazine, 2008.
8. Hamerschlag and Strochlic. *Best Labor Practices on Twelve California Farms: Towards a More Sustainable Food System*. California Institute for Rural Studies, 2006.
9. USDA, 2007 Census of Agriculture, Table 45, p. 49.
10. Nabhan, *Enduring Seeds*.

CHAPTER 5

1. U.S. Census Bureau, "Annual Estimates of the Population of Metropolitan and Micropolitan Statistical Areas" (accessed June 29, 2009).
2. Morgan, "Farm Bill Passes by Veto Proof Margins" (accessed June 29, 2009).
3. People's Grocery, "About West Oakland" (accessed June 29, 2009).
4. Wooten and Unger, "Oakland Food Systems Assessment" (accessed June 29, 2009).
5. Ibid.
6. People's Grocery, "About West Oakland" (accessed June 29, 2009).
7. Ibid.
8. USDA, 2007 Census of Agriculture.
9. Finnin, City Slicker Farms Annual Report.

CHAPTER 6

1. USDA, 2007 Census of Agriculture.
2. The Greenhorns, "The Greenhorn Guidebook" (accessed May 5, 2009).
3. USDA, 2007 Census of Agriculture.

APPENDIX A

1. Kotschi and Müller-Sämann, *The Role of Organic Agriculture in Mitigating Climate Change.*
2. Ibid.
3. Gurian-Sherman, "Failure to Yield" (accessed June 29, 2009).
4. Food and Agriculture Organization of the United Nations, "Climate Change Mitigation."
5. El-Hage Scialabba and Hattam, *Organic Agriculture, Environment, and Food Security.*
6. Klein, Kregs, Hall, O'Brien, and Blevins, *California's Water-Energy Relationship.*
7. Kotschi and Müller-Sämann, *The Role of Organic Agriculture in Mitigating Climate Change.*

RESOURCES

THE WOMEN OF FARMER JANE

Leigh Adcock (page 135)
Executive Director
Women, Food and
  Agriculture Network
PO Box 611
Ames, IA 50010
515.460.2477
leigh@wfan.org
www.wfan.org

Erika Allen (page 165)
Chicago Projects Manager
Growing Power Chicago
2215 W. North Avenue
Chicago, IL 60647
773.486.6005
erika@growingpower.org
www.growingpower.org

Zoë Bradbury (page 194)
Valley Flora Farm
Blog: Diary of a Young Farmer,
  www.edibleportland.com
www.valleyflorafarm.com

Jo Ann Baumgartner (page 150)
Executive Director
Wild Farm Alliance
info@wildfarm.org
www.wildfarmalliance.org

Renata Brillinger (page 204)
Executive Director
California Climate &
  Agriculture Network
707.874.0316
renata@calclimateag.org
www.calclimateag.org

Novella Carpenter (page 180)
www.ghosttownfarm.wordpress.com
www.biofueloasis.com

Jesse Cool (page 117)
Flea St. Cafe
Cool Cafe, Stanford
Cool Cafe, Menlo Business Park
650.854.5806
admin@cooleatz.com
www.cooleatz.com

Claire Hope Cummings (page 55)
claire@clairehopecummings.com
www.clairehopecummings.com

Gloria Decater (page 41)
Live Power Community Farm
Covelo, CA 95428
707.983.8196
info@livepower.org
www.livepower.org

Lois Ellen Frank (page 121)
505.466.6306
lois@redmesacuisine.com
www.redmesacuisine.com
www.loisphoto.com

**Jessica Greenblatt
Seeley** (page 137)
FoodRoutes Network &
  Milky Way Farms
RR #1 Box 25
Troy, PA 16947
570.673.3398
jess@foodroutes.org
www.foodroutes.org
www.milkywayfarms.net

Elizabeth Henderson (page 21)
Peacework Farm
2218 Welcher Road
Newark, NY 14513
315.331.9029
elizabethhenderson13@gmail.com

Glenda Humiston, Ph.D. (page 73)
humiston@nature.berkeley.edu

Marion Kalb (page 81)
Community Food Security Coalition
P.O. Box 4877
Santa Fe, NM 87502
505.474.5782
marion@foodsecurity.org
www.foodsecurity.org

Deborah Koons Garcia (page 68)
Lily Films
P.O. Box 895
Mill Valley, CA 94942
800.981.7870
info@lilyfilms.com
www.thefutureoffood.com

Anna Blythe Lappé (page 63)
Small Planet Institute
anna@smallplanet.org
www.smallplanet.org
www.takeabite.cc

Deborah Madison (page 94)
deborahmadison@earthlink.net
www.randomhouse.com/
   features/deborahmadison

Traci Miller (page 113)
L'Etoile Restaurant and Café Soleil
25 North Pinckney Street
Madison, WI 53703
608.251.0500
fabfrenchfood@yahoo.com
www.letoile-restaurant.com

Melissa Nelson (page 156)
The Cultural Conservancy
P.O. Box 29044
San Francisco, CA 94129
415.561.6594
mknelson@igc.org
www.earthdiver.org

Denise O'Brien (page 130)
Rolling Acres Farm
Women, Food and
   Agriculture Network
P.O. Box 611
Ames, IA 50010
hnob@metc.net
www.wfan.org

Emily Oakley (page 36)
Three Springs Farm
1367 Highway 82A
Oaks, OK 74359
918.868.5450
farmers@threespringsfarm.com
www.threespringsfarm.com

Jessica Prentice (page 100)
Three Stone Hearth
jessica@threestonehearth.com
www.threestonehearth.com
www.localfoodswheel.com
www.locavores.com

Dru Rivers (page 28)
Full Belly Farm
530.796.2214
dru@fullbellyfarm.com
www.fullybellyfarm.com

Willow Rosenthal (page 173)
willow@cityslickerfarms.org
www.cityslickerfarms.org

Olivia Sargeant (page 115)
Farm 225
255 W. Washington Street
Athens, GA
706.549.4660
www.farm255.com

Mily Treviño-Sauceda (page 144)
Organización en CA de Líderes
   Campesinas, Inc.
761 S. C St.
Oxnard, CA 93030
805.486.7776
liderescampesinas@hotmail.com
www.líderescampesinas.org

**Severine von Tscharner
Fleming** (page 190)
www.thegreenhorns.net
http://smithereenfarm.word
   press.com

Nancy Vail (page 13)
Pie Ranch
Pescadero, CA
nancy@pieranch.org
www.pieranch.org

Judy Wicks (page 105)
White Dog Cafe
3420 Sansom St.
Philadelphia, PA 19104
judy@whitedog.com
www.whitedog.com
www.livingeconomies.org
www.sbnPhiladelphia.rog
www.judywicks.com

Aimee Witteman (page 207)
National Sustainable
   Agriculture Coalition
202.547.5754
awitteman@
   sustainableagriculture.net
www.sustainableagriculture.net

WEBSITES

For more information, visit www.
farmerjane.org for current links
on the following topics regarding
women and sustainable agriculture.

Women and Sustainable Food and Farming Organizations

Find regional, national and
international women and
sustainable food and agriculture
organizations. Connect locally
or plug into a bigger network.

National Organizations for Sustainable Food and Farms

Here you'll find links to national
centers of resources throughout
the United States.

Farm Worker Organizations

This page provides resources for
farm worker organizations, both
national and international.

Indigenous Foods and Food Culture

Find out resources to connect
with people that are actively
preserving indigenous food
and culture throughout the
United States and beyond.

Local Food

Find information on where to access
local food guides and other online
resources, as well as organizations
and initiatives that are promoting
local foods throughout the country.

Sustainable Agriculture

Need some background on sustainable food and agriculture in general? This list of websites will link you direct to the pros such as the Environmental Working Group, Food and Water Watch, and Center for Food Safety.

Seed/Heirloom Saving Organizations and Organizations Against Genetically Modified Foods

Want to know where to get your hands on heirloom varieties of seeds or even heritage varieties of animals? Go to this page while learning about genetic engineering dangers in the process.

Policy and Advocacy Organizations

Farm Bill policy in the United States is undoubtedly behind the transition to industrial foods, not only in the U.S. but the world over. The organizations found here are working for progressive, sustainably minded food policies in the U.S. and beyond.

Farm to School

These organizations are teaching kids that potatoes and carrots come from the ground—not from a plastic bag.

Advocacy Organizations for Sustainable Food Businesses

While nonprofits have their niche in pushing a new sustainable food agenda, for-profit businesses do too in putting their money where their mouths are. This page highlights business collaboratives with a mission for local, sustainable, and socially responsible foods.

Food Policy Councils

Many cities are developing food policy councils to create policies that ensure affordable, healthy, and culturally appropriate food for all. These councils serve to connect organizations, individuals and policy makers working to change the food system, and to assess the needs in local communities. Their work includes planning for agriculture within cities as well as fostering connections between urban eaters and rural agriculture. This list is as comprehensive as possible, although new policy councils are sprouting up often.

Soil Testing

If you live in an urban area and are thinking of growing food, you should get your soil tested first. Visit this page for links to where you can find soil testing.

Urban Farming and Gardening

The list that you'll find is by no means exhaustive; in fact, there are more urban farms and gardens than ever! See if your town is represented and contact us at info@farmerjane.org if it isn't.

The following books are indispensable. In addition, numerous institutions—UW Wisconsin, Madison, Universidad Austral de Chile, UC Davis (UC SAREP, Small Farm Center, Student Farm and Garden)—along with conversations with individuals over the last decade have contributed to *Farmer Jane*'s formation. For additional resources and links to organizations related to the book, please visit www.farmerjane.org.

CANNING AND PRESERVING FOODS
Chadwick, Janet. *The Busy Person's Guide to Preserving Food: Easy Step-by-Step Instructions for Freezing, Drying, and Canning.* North Adams, MA: Storey, 1995.
The Gardeners and Farmers of Terra Vivante. *Preserving Food without Freezing or Canning: Traditional Techniques Using Salt, Oil, Sugar, Alcohol, Vinegar, Drying, Cold Storage, and Lactic Fermentation.* White River Junction, VT: Chelsea Green, 1999.
Katz, Sandor Ellix. *Wild Fermentation: The Flavor, Nutrition and Craft of Live Culture Foods.* White River Junction, VT: Chelsea Green, 2003.

COMMUNITY SUPPORTED AGRICULTURE
Henderson, Elizabeth, with Robyn Van En. *Sharing the Harvest: A Citizen's Guide to Community Supported Agriculture.* White River Junction, VT: Chelsea Green, 2003.

COOKBOOKS
Cool, Jesse. *Simply Organic.* San Francisco, CA: Chronicle Books, 2000 and 2008.
———. *The True and Real One Pot Cookbook.* San Francisco, CA: Chronicle Books, 2006.
———. *Your Organic Kitchen.* Emmaus, PA: Rodale Press, 2000.
Fisher, M.F.K. *How to Cook a Wolf.* San Francisco, CA: North Point Press, 1988.
Frank, Lois Ellen. *Foods of the Southwest Indian Nations.* Berkeley, CA: Ten Speed Press, 2003.
———. *Native American Cooking: Foods of the Southwest Indian Nations.* Berkeley, CA: Ten Speed Press, 2002.
———. *The Taco Table: Contemporary Tacos from a Chef's Kitchen using Local, Sustainable and Fresh Ingredients.* Tucson, AZ: Western National Parks Association, 2010.
Lappé, Anna, and Bryant Terry. *Grub: Ideas for an Urban Organic Kitchen.* New York: Tarcher/Penguin, 2006.
Madison, Deborah, and Patrick McFarlin. *What We Eat When We Eat Alone.* Layton, UT: Gibbs Smith, 2009.
Madison, Deborah. *The Greens Cookbook.* New York: Broadway, 2001.
———. *Local Flavors.* New York: Broadway, 2002.
———. *Seasonal Fruit Desserts: From Orchard, Farm, and Market.* New York: Broadway, 2010.
———. *Vegetarian Cooking for Everyone.* New York: Broadway, 1997.
Nelson, Davia, and Nikki Silva. *Hidden Kitchens.* Emmaus, PA: Rodale Books, 2006.

Prentice, Jessica. *Full Moon Feast: Food and the Hunger for Connection.* White River Junction, VT: Chelsea Green, 2006.

Waters, Alice. *The Art of Simple Food.* New York, NY: Clarkson Potter, 2007.

———. *Edible Schoolyard: A Universal Idea.* San Francisco, CA: Chronicle Books, 2008.

———. *Chez Panisse Menu Cookbook.* New York, NY: Random House, 1995.

Wicks, Judy, and Kevin von Klause. *The White Dog Café Cookbook: Multicultural Recipes and Tales of Adventure from Philadelphia's Revolutionary Restaurant.* Philadelphia, PA: Running Press, 1998.

FARM BUSINESS

Eat Well Guide. "Cultivating the Web: High Tech Tools for the Sustainable Food Movement." eatwellguide.org.

Feenstra, Gail, Jeri Ohmart, and David Chaney. "Selling Directly to Restaurants and Retailers." Davis, CA: University of California Sustainable Agriculture Research Program; 2003.

SEEDS

Ashworth, Suzanne. *Seed to Seed: Seed Saving and Growing Techniques for Vegetable Gardeners.* Decorah, IA: Seed Savers Exchange, 2002.

Cummings, Claire Hope. *Uncertain Peril: Genetic Engineering and the Future of Seeds.* Boston, MA: Beacon Press, 2008.

Nabhan, Gary Paul. *Enduring Seeds: Native American Agriculture and Wild Plant Conservation.* Tucson, AZ: University of Arizona Press, 2002.

SUSTAINABLE FOOD

Berry, Wendell. *The Unsettling of America.* San Francisco, CA: Sierra Club Books, 1977.

Cook, Christopher C. *Diet for a Dead Planet.* New York, NY: New Press, 2006.

Fernald, Anya, Serena Milano, and Piero Sardo, eds. *A World of Presidia: Food, Culture, and Community.* Bra, Italy: Slow Food Editore, 2004.

Food and Agriculture Organization of the United Nations. "A Matter of Survival: FAO promotes unique international treaty on agricultural diversity." FAO in Action. Food and Agriculture Organization of the United Nations: 2002. http://www.fao.org/english/newsroom/action/pdf/ag_treaty.pdf (accessed June 29, 2009).

———. "Climate change mitigation and adaptation in agriculture, forestry and fisheries." June 2008. http://www.fao.org/foodclimate/conference/doclist/en/?no_cache=1.

Gurian-Sherman, Doug. "Failure to Yield: Evaluating the Performance of Genetically Engineered Crops." Union of Concerned Scientists: 2009. http://www.ucsusa.org/food_and_agriculture/science_and_impacts/science/failure-to-yield.htmls (accessed June 29, 2009).

Hamerschlag, Kari, and Strochlic, Ron. "Best Labor Practices on Twelve California Farms: Towards a More Sustainable Food System." Davis, CA: California Institute for Rural Studies, 2006. Available at www.cirsinc.org.

Hawken, Paul. *Blessed Unrest: How the Largest Social Movement in History is Restoring Grace, Justice, and Beauty to the World.* New York, NY: Penguin, 2008.

Katz, Sandor Ellix. *The Revolution Will Not Be Microwaved*. White River Junction, VT: Chelsea Green, 2006.

Kimbrell, Andrew, ed. *Fatal Harvest: The Tragedy of Industrial Agriculture*. Sausalito, CA: Foundation for Deep Ecology, 2002.

Lappé, Anna, and Frances Moore Lappé. *Hope's Edge*. New York: Tarcher/Penguin, 2002.

Lappé, Anna. *Diet for a Hot Planet: The Climate Crisis at the End of Our Fork and What We Can Do About It*. London: Bloomsbury, 2010.

Martineau, Belinda. *First Fruit: The Creation of the Flavr Savr Tomato and the Birth of Biotech Foods*. Columbus, OH: McGraw-Hill Companies, 2001.

Nabhan, Gary. *Coming Home to Eat: The Pleasures and Politics of Local Foods*. New York, NY: Norton, W.W. & Company, 2002.

————. *Renewing America's Food Traditions: Saving and Savoring the Continent's Most Endangered Foods*. White River Junction, VT: Chelsea Green, 2008.

————. *Why Some Like it Hot: Food, Genes, and Cultural Diversity*. Washington D.C.: Island Press, 2006.

————. *Where our Food Comes From: Retracing Nikolay Vavilov's Quest to End Famine*. Washington D.C.: Island Press, 2008.

Nestle, Marion. *Food Politics*. Berkeley, CA: University of California, 2003.

————. *What to Eat*. New York, NY: North Point Press, 2006.

Patel, Raj. *Stuffed and Starved: The Hidden Battle for the World's Food System*. New York, NY: HarperCollins, 2009.

————. *Food Rebellions: Crisis and the Hunger for Justice*. Oakland, CA: Food First, 2009.

Pollan, Michael. *Omnivore's Dilemma: The Natural History of Four Meals*. New York, NY: Penguin Press, 2006.

————. *In Defense of Food*. New York, NY: Penguin Press, 2008.

Vilesisis, Ann. *Kitchen Literacy: How We Lost Knowledge of Where Food Comes From and Why We Need to Get It Back*. Washington, D.C.: Island Press, 2008

URBAN FARMING

Carpenter, Novella, and Rosenthal, Willow. *The Essential Urban Farmer*. New York: Penguin Press, 2010.

Carpenter, Novella. *Farm City: The Education of an Urban Farmer*. New York: Penguin Press, 2009.

Flores, Heather C. *Food Not Lawns: How to Turn Your Yard into a Garden and Your Neighborhood into a Community*. White River Junction, VT: Chelsea Green, 2006.

Javits, Tom, Helga and Bill Olkowski, and the Farallones Institute Staff. *The Integral Urban House: Self-Reliant Living in the City*. San Francisco, CA: Sierra Club Books, 1979

INDEX